The Jewish Role in American Life

An Annual Review

The Jewish Role in American Life

An Annual Review

Volume 1

Barry Glassner

Hilary Taub Lachoff

Tom Teicholz

USC Casden Institute for the Study of the Jewish Role in American Life
Los Angeles

ISBN 0-9717400-0-3

Book design by John Banner.
Set in Times New Roman.
Printed on Cascade 60 lb. offset.

Printed in the United States of America by
KNI, Incorporated, Anaheim, California.

Published by the USC Casden Institute for the Study of the
Jewish Role in American Life
University of Southern California,
Grace Ford Salvatori Hall, Room 304,
Los Angeles, California 90089-1697

Contents

Acknowledgements

This volume represents the collaborative efforts of many people, over many months. We would like to expressly thank a few of these individuals, without whom this project would not have been possible. First, we'd like to thank Alan Casden for his generous support of this publication and the Casden Institute for the Study of the Jewish Role in American Life. We also thank the members of the Casden Institute Advisory Board, many of whom were founding members, and all of whom advise and support the Casden Institute in each of our efforts. They are: Lewis Barth, Mark Benjamin, Joseph Bentley, Alan Berlin, Jonathan Brandler, Michael Diamond, Solomon Golomb, Jonathan Klein, Ray Kurtzman, Susan Laemmle, Marlene Adler Marks, Beth Meyerowitz, Michael Renov, Cara Robertson, Chip Robertson, Carol Brennglass Spinner, Scott Stone, Ruth Weisberg and Ruth Ziegler. We'd like to thank the University of Southern California, USC President Steven B. Sample, Provost Lloyd Armstrong and Joseph Aoun, Dean of the USC College of Letters, Arts and Sciences, for their continued support and for providing the intellectual and cultural environment in which we thrive. Finally, thanks to Elisabeth Finch for copy editing, Rick Ventura and Susan Wilcox for Development operations and Martha Harris for excellent editorial suggestions.

Introduction

The American Jewish community has had a profound influence on the United States, playing a vital role in areas as diverse as commerce, law, education, politics, philanthropy and the arts. Although the history of Jews in America stretches back before the founding of this nation, the Jewish role in American life is ever evolving. The mission of the Casden Institute for the Study of the Jewish Role in American Life is to support research that aims to spur dialogue and achieve greater understanding not only about what it means to be Jewish in America but what it means to be American in a pluralistic society. To that end we have produced this volume, our annual scholarly report, which examines various aspects of the Jewish role in American life.

At the Casden Institute, there is a commitment to explore not only our heritage but also our future. Accordingly, this book relies on both scholarly and popular literature. Our approach is academic, while our sources are contemporary. Each year we will take a fresh look at the Jewish role in American life, examining different areas of interest and concern.

In this, our first volume, we selected five key areas: politics, culture, values, education and image. We reviewed leading scholarly and popular sources within each area, focusing on issues of contemporary concern. Drawing from these sources, we hope to provide an analysis of what American Jews are thinking, saying, studying and doing in these key fields.

In each chapter, we synthesize issues vital to an understanding of the Jewish experience in our times. In the politics chapter, we examine the tradition of liberalism among American Jews, the candidacy of Senator Joseph Lieberman for vice president of the United States, and the politicization of Jewish organizations, women's associations and new immigrants. In our chapter on culture, we explore cultural institutions and the search for a Jewish idiom in three distinct arenas: art museums, music and popular musical theater. In the values chapter, we identify new organizations and new initiatives in giving that reflect trends in the Jewish population as a whole. In the education chapter, we discuss several approaches to ensuring Jewish continuity in the 21st century, including the evolution of Jewish attendance at public and private schools, Jewish education at day schools and in Sunday and Hebrew schools and the debate over school vouchers. Finally, our image chapter charts the changing self-image of Jews as presented in contemporary literature by a new generation of writers who write about being Jewish.

These chapters are meant to challenge our assumptions and chronicle the changes occurring within the Jewish community. We ask difficult questions: Are American Jews remaining liberal, or are we moving to the right? Why are we philanthropic? Is Jewish participation in the arts motivated by a desire to assimilate? Is there such a thing as Jewish music? Why are we, as Jews, so committed to public education? Should we support school vouchers? How do we combat assimilation and intermarriage? Is there a difference between writers who are Jewish and Jewish writing?

Although these questions may appear, at first, disparate, core themes resonate across the chapters. The common thread in all these chapters is a recognition that we are living in a time of pluralistic Judaism, a time when it is acceptable to turn inward and focus more on being Jewish, without any stigma that doing so makes us any less American. Our survey reveals that over the last century, American Jews have embraced American institutions and art forms, arriving at the very summit of achievement in every field. Each chapter is, in some small way, a chronicle of the overwhelming success of American Jews in the last century. Consider a few examples: A modern Orthodox Jew, Senator Joseph Lieberman, was the first Jewish vice presidential candidate of a major political party. The United Jewish Communities was listed as the seventh largest philanthropic organization in the United States. In Los Angeles, Jewish donors created several major cultural art institutions in the last 40 years. In the music world, American Jews have played a major role as executives and have achieved unparalleled success as singers, songwriters and performers of popular music, be it as conductors and composers of classical music, as jazz artists or as rock performers. In the musical theater, the most successful recent play is Mel Brooks' "The Producers," a Jewish-identified work, while at the same time the more traditional and sentimental "Fiddler on the Roof" continues to tour. Jewish American literature, which blossomed from a generation of immigrants' children intent on exploring the friction that occurred as they assimilated, almost succeeded so well as to leave nothing more to say. Nonetheless, a whole new generation of writers has arrived to provide new images of Jews in contemporary America.

Our survey concludes that Jews have so successfully become part of the fabric of American life, they can feel free to explore and express their Judaism. Consequently, there is a flowering of Jewish self-expression that we uncover throughout all of the chapters. This freedom of self-expression is exemplified in our politics chapter by a vice presidential candidate who wears a yarmulke and recent Russian immigrants who have become politicized; in our culture chapter, by the search for a specifically Jewish idiom in music, the explosion of Jewish alternative music and a shamelessly Jewish play; in philanthropy, there are new initiatives and new organizations that have been created to foster Jewish identity in trips to Israel and even a singles concert hall and club in New York; in our education chapter, we highlight the proliferation of Jewish day schools and the call for a new vision for the 21st century for supplemental Jewish education; in our image chapter, we feature a whole new generation of writers who write not about the American experience so much as their reactions to things Jewish, as gays, children of survivors and immigrants. Together, these chapters create a mosaic of the Jewish role in American life.

More specifically, each of our chapters explores core issues. From our very first chapter, on politics, we discuss the extent to which American Jews define themselves through political action. We explore the various possible explanations that scholars and popular writers have suggested for the long-standing tradition of liberalism among American Jews, including Judaic, political, historical and sociological reasons as well as loyalty to the institution of the Democratic Party. This allegiance to social action, liberalism and to the Democratic Party remains as true for today's Russian immigrants as it did for the immigrants of a century ago. This does not mean that all Jews are liberal, or that all Jews who vote Democratic in national elections are liberal on all issues. Many theories have been offered to explain the phenomenon of Jewish liberalism; however, many scholars observe that those Jews who stand in a liberal position toward Judaism tend to be more liberal on social issues than those Jews who practice their religion in a more Orthodox manner. American Jews' commitment to political action is present in its Federations, women's organizations, local agencies and even its newest immigrants. The connection between American Jews and politics continues to thrive. Finally, we take special interest in the candidacy of Senator Joseph Lieberman for vice president of the United States during Election 2000, very tangible evidence of what American Jews have achieved in the political process.

In a similar vein, our chapter on culture records the ways in which, over the last century, American Jews have succeeded at the highest level, making tremendous contributions to American culture. There are a number of American Jews who have emerged as significant collectors, donors and directors at many of the country's most important art museums, including Boston's Fogg

Museum, New York's Metropolitan Museum of Art, Museum of Modern Art, Guggenheim Museum, Whitney Museum of American Art and the New Museum. Forty years ago, Los Angeles was barren of significant museums or facilities to showcase modern art. Today, partly because of the efforts of a small group of local Jewish collectors and museum officials, there are more than a half dozen major institutions in the greater Los Angeles area, such as the Los Angeles County Museum of Art (LACMA), the Norton Simon Museum, the Museum of Contemporary Art (MOCA), the Hammer/UCLA Museum, the Museum of Tolerance, the Skirball Cultural Center and the Getty Museum.

We also note the extent to which American Jews have reached unparalleled levels of fame and achievement in the world of music. In the 1930s, Benny Goodman helped jazz become the most popular music in the country. In the rock era, beginning in the late 1950s and continuing until the present, Jewish singers, songwriters and musicians were absorbed by the popular culture, even as they changed their names to do so. American Jews continue to play important roles as executives and artists, but there is a new generation that is more vocal about their heritage. Today, a number of artists are engaged in a vital exploration of Jewish music in a variety of forms. Jewish alternative music, for example, draws record crowds of Jews and non-Jews all over the country and all over the world. Finally, in the world of musical theater, two musicals, both with Jewish characteristics but with very different attitudes, are currently being performed: "Fiddler on the Roof" and "The Producers." One is sentimental about its Jewish context, the other is brazen; both delight audiences of Jews and non-Jews alike. Our survey concludes that at the beginning of the 21st century, American Jews have achieved the highest levels of acceptance and success from cultural institutions and, as artists, from the rest of the culture by virtue of their talent. They have no need to hide their heritage and are freer than ever to use and explore Jewish themes.

The creativity and innovation that we detail in the chapter on culture is also apparent as we survey the world of philanthropy in our values chapter. It will come as no surprise to find that American Jews continue to express a deep and sincere commitment to charity and philanthropy. Yet the reasons and ways we give are worth exploring. Inspired by Jewish concepts of *tzedakah* and *tikkun olam*, there is a long tradition of giving, which exists to this day. Jewish charitable organizations such as the Federations, created at the beginning of the previous century to provide social services for immigrants and the UJA, created to rescue Jews from World War II, have merged to form the United Jewish Communities (UJC). Its daunting task is to correct the mistakes of the past and make choices for the future. Criticized in the past for being unresponsive and uncreative, the UJC faces a new landscape of donors and philanthropy. Individual donors want more control over where their funds go. Jewish philanthropy must look to the future, emphasizing positive messages, focusing on Jewish education and creating new initiatives for funders to express themselves Jewishly.

The question of how to encourage Jewish identity is central to our education chapter. In our exploration of current scholarship and contemporary concerns, we found that education continues to be a major concern for most Americans in general and Jews in particular. A century ago, the fear that immigrant children would be absorbed into the melting pot and lose their Jewish identity was the cause for the creation of supplemental Sunday school education and, following that, Hebrew School. We review scholars, commentators and others engaged in issues of Jewish education not only at the parochial level but as they interface with such national issues as school choice and school vouchers. Although intermarriage and assimilation pose real threats to Jewish identity and continuity, our survey reviews the development of Jewish education in America and the allegiance to public education, and we set this in the context of ways to ensure Jewish continuity in the 21st century.

Finally, our survey asks: Who are those American Jews who are exploring, defining and presenting to the rest of society a Jewish image? What can we learn from them about the Jewish role in American society? In examining Jewish self-image as revealed in contemporary literature, we conclude that, to paraphrase Mark Twain, the reports of the death of Jewish American literature were greatly exaggerated. The scholars and writers we cite are witness to a renaissance of Jewish American writing. We are seeing works about Judaism in all its iterations, from the Hasidic world to the Reform. There are imaginative works about shtetl life, Israel and the worlds of the new immigrants. Contemporary American Jewish writers are exploring the margins of American Jewish society, writing about gay Jews, children of Holocaust survivors, pious Jews — all subsets within the Jewish community — but they are doing so for the mainstream and presenting to all Americans a new image of American Jews.

These chapters show the great extent to which American Jews are richly engaged in the life of this nation. As Americans, as Jews, as standard bearers for the Jewish role in American life, our accomplishments are remarkable. Even those critics who perceive a crisis in Jewish identity, education or continuity make these arguments to a large audience of interested parties. The mere fact these arguments are being made in popular and scholarly volumes speaks loudly to the health and strength of the Jewish community. If critics worried that we, as American Jews, would disappear, these five chapters provide a resounding response.

With this volume, the Casden Institute identifies and examines the Jewish role in American life and the issues raised by recent scholarly, academic and popular essays. It is an ambitious undertaking, and hence, a few caveats are in order. First, we do not intend for the chapters in this first volume to cover the full range of areas in which Jews are making important contributions to American life. For example, even as we discuss in this volume a variety of topics relating to the arts and literature, we save for next year's edition a discussion of cinema, an area of great interest to the Casden Institute. Over the past few years, we have organized several successful conferences and screenings on Jewish autobiography through film and on the treatment of the Holocaust in film.

Second, while it is not our intention to present ourselves as the single authority on any of these subjects, our hope is to add our voice to those interested in the course of Jewish events in America. To that end, we acknowledge other important works that survey the American Jewish experience and are aimed at a general readership rather than experts, in particular, *The American Jewish Yearbook*. In its 2000 edition, the *Yearbook* traces its long journey over the last century and the evolution that has brought it to its current state of authority. It is our hope to complement the well-respected and comprehensive statistical and scholarly data found in those volumes, with our own far more modest contributions.

At the same time, we believe that the Casden Institute's scholarly orientation and contemporary focus, combined with its location on the West Coast, give us a unique vantage point to explore those areas and issues where the Jewish community interfaces with the broader concerns and cultures that form the nation. We are cognizant of the enormity of the task we have set for ourselves. We at the Casden Institute are eager to meet this challenge as we pursue our mission. We do so partly through these annual volumes and partly by hosting conferences and symposia that feature eminent scholars and leaders from business, government, the media and the arts, and by supporting and promoting original scholarship and research. We host special programs and interdepartmental events, such as film series and museum presentations, to educate large numbers of college students and community members about the American Jewish experience.

In a sense, these annual volumes function as forums in which we pause to reflect, gathering both academic and popular sources for our review. In the subjects we cover, the issues we address and the sources we cite, we seek to create a portrait of American Jews in the 21st century. This portrait is an evolving mosaic and we hope that readers will find it lively, thought provoking and engaging. Like a Seder, we intend to convene yearly to remind ourselves of what we have been through, to ponder our greatest challenges and to celebrate our most significant achievements. In the end, if we have succeeded, we will have contributed to our understanding of Jewish life in America and what it means to be American.

Chapter One

POLITICS:
A Tradition of Liberalism

The American Jewish community has a long liberal tradition that expresses itself not only in consistent voting patterns at both the national and local level, but also in our commitment to social and political action through Jewish institutions and agencies. American Jews continue to be more liberal than most Americans and more liberal than most minorities of a similar social and economic make-up. However, there is a long tradition of conservatism and we will explore whether or not American Jews are moving to the right.

In this chapter, we will discuss the many possible reasons for American Jewish liberalism, including Judaic, political, historical and sociological reasons, as well as an allegiance to the institution of the Democratic Party. In the end, however, Jewish liberalism may have more to do with Jewish attitudes toward religion than anything else. Orthodox Jews tend to support the status quo; Jews who take a more liberal position

1

toward their own religion also seem to take a more liberal position toward society.

In this light, we will pay special attention to the candidacy of Senator Joseph Lieberman for vice president of the United States. The selection of the first Jewish candidate on a major party presidential ticket was an epochal event for American Jews, but perhaps even more so for Orthodox Jews. In Election 2000, the choice of Senator Lieberman as the Democratic candidate for vice president may have been more a function of his conservative positions than his Orthodox practices.

Political expression and participation by American Jews occur not only in national elections but also in the subsets of our community, among new immigrants and even among their institutions, even if such organizations are characterized as "women's charitable organizations" such as Hadassah. American Jewish liberalism is expressed in the political agendas of Jewish institutions and organizations, yet scholars find this does not compromise their effectiveness. On the contrary, local Jewish agencies such as the New York Association for New Americans, Inc. (NYANA) have found a way to have a profound impact on a national level on issues of resettlement and immigration.

Accordingly, we begin this chapter with the facts and statistics documenting the tradition of Jewish support for presidential candidates from the Democratic Party. We will discuss, in further detail, American Jewish liberalism and the history of conservatism, the Lieberman candidacy and the political engagement of subsets and communities within the American Jewish experience.

A Desire for Inclusion? Historical Support and Statistics

For most of the century, beginning with Theodore Roosevelt's ascension to the presidency in 1901 following the assassination of President McKinley, American Jews have supported a progressive and liberal agenda.[1]

---

[1] Marc Dollinger, *Quest for Inclusion: Jews and Liberalism in Modern America* (New Jersey: Princeton University Press, 2000): 9.

This political allegiance has been strongly defined by support for the Democratic Party. In 1932, 82% of Jewish voters cast their support for Franklin Roosevelt; in 1940, 90% voted for Franklin Roosevelt; in 1948, 90% of Jews voted for Harry S. Truman or Wendell Willkie; by contrast in 1952, only 36% voted for Eisenhower, and in 1956 only 40%. In 1960, John F. Kennedy garnered 88% of the Jewish vote (Kennedy only won 81% of the Roman Catholic vote); 90% voted for Lyndon Johnson in 1964; and in 1968, 81% voted for Hubert Humphrey rather than Richard Nixon. In 1972, when Nixon ran against McGovern, McGovern earned only 65% of the Jewish vote. In 1976, Carter earned the same 65%, which declined even further in the 1980 race against Reagan, when the combined Carter and Anderson Jewish vote tallied 61%. Reagan's 39% in 1980 was a high water mark for a Republican candidate, declining to 31% in 1984. In 1988, Michael Dukakis won 88% of the Jewish vote against George H.W. Bush. In 1992, when Bush won only 12% of the Jewish vote, Ross Perot garnered 10%. In 1996, Clinton was reelected with 81% of the Jewish vote.[2]

In addition, from 1933-1975, Jewish liberalism had a large and profound influence on such issues as the New Deal, the creation of the United Nations, pleas for pluralism during the McCarthy era and Lyndon Johnson's "Great Society" policies.[3]

How do we explain such loyalty? In his book *Quest for Inclusion: Jews and Liberalism in Modern America*, Marc Dollinger puts forward the thesis that Jews are motivated not by liberalism but by a desire to be included in the fabric of American life.[4] Yet when there is a clash between liberalism and Jewish interests, Dollinger maintains that Jews have almost always chosen the latter.[5] However, as we will show, many other theories have been offered to explore American Jews' political stance — each flawed in its own way.

[2] Edward S. Shapiro, "Liberal Politics and the Jewish Identity," *Judaism* 47.4.188 (1998): 430.
[3] Paul Barton-Kriese, "Review of Marc Dollinger's *Quest for Inclusion: Jews and Liberalism in Modern America*," *Perspectives on Political Science* 301.1 (2001): 49.
[4] Barton-Kriese 49.
[5] Dollinger 4.

A Tradition of Liberalism or a Move to the Right?

Although the history of American Jewish liberalism stretches back for more than a century, the reasons for this pattern remain difficult to explain. Many theories have been offered:

1. *The Jewish Values Argument*: Jews are liberal because of an adherence to Judaic values and traditions.
2. *The Historical Argument*: A long history of oppression and persecution in Western Europe causes Jews to view their emancipation as going hand in hand with a quest for social equality.
3. *The Political Argument*: There are a number of issues of concern to American Jews that, when aggregated, form the basis of a liberal agenda.
4. *The Sociological Argument*: It is American Jews' status as a minority that causes them to make common cause with liberals.
5. *The Institutional Argument*: Jewish liberalism may be more a matter of loyalty to the institution of the Democratic Party than a matter of personal conviction.

In the end, each of these arguments does not explain the liberalism of American Jews. Orthodox Jews — who adhere closest to core Jewish tenets, share a history of political persecution, and remain outsiders — are the least liberal and often espouse conservative values and politics. Accordingly, a different rationale may explain this phenomenon. American Jews are not a monolithic group, voting differently on specific issues and differently in state and local elections than in national ones. Although American Jews continue to vote overwhelmingly Democratic, there exists a long tradition of conservatism that cannot be denied. We will examine each of these arguments before we review possible ways to reconcile the findings in our survey.

The Jewish Values Argument. Jewish liberalism is often explained as hewing to core Jewish values of *"tzedakah"* (charity and social justice) and "*gemilut hasidim*" (acts of loving-kindness).[6] Others cite "*torah*" (education) and the mandate to enjoy one's life on Earth rather than lead an ascetic path in hopes of a world to come.[7]

Although these may be good reasons to follow a liberal agenda, they do not explain the consistency of the Jewish liberal position throughout a century of social and cultural change. Moreover, as Geoffrey Levey points out, Orthodox observant groups are often more conservative politically. Therefore, Jewish principles or Judaic values do not, in themselves, account for the political allegiance of the majority of American Jews.[8]

The Historical Argument. Another theory is that American Jews are liberal for historical reasons. The Jews' history of persecution, together with their struggle for rights in Europe, it is argued, has led them to consistently support a progressive and liberal agenda.[9] To the Jews who were confined to ghettos in medieval times, and who suffered state-sponsored segregation and anti-Semitism that limited their social mobility and economic opportunities, the enlightenment offered the promise of Jewish civil equality.[10] Historically, Jews lacked power in Europe; to alleviate their condition, they envisaged a radical restructuring of society.[11] In essence, Jews adopted liberal ideas hand in hand with their own emancipation.[12]

The problem with this theory is that it does not consider why it is that Jews wanted emancipation.[13] In many cases, emancipation came at the cost of giving up religious or communal values. To become a member of European society often meant assimilating. In France, for example, Napoleon wanted Jews to be French, not Jewish.[14] This raises a difficult question: Which is paramount for the Jewish community, a drive toward

---

[6] Dollinger 7.
[7] Geoffrey Brahm Levey, "The Liberalism of American Jews – Has It Been Explained," *British Journal of Political Science* 26 (1996): 375.
[8] Levey 375.
[9] Levey 375.
[10] Dollinger 8.
[11] Shapiro 430.
[12] Dollinger 8.
[13] Levey 375.
[14] Shapiro 430.

liberalism or a drive to assimilate into the dominant culture? As Edward Shapiro points out, in the end, instead of achieving their goals of equality, Jews immigrated in large numbers to the West.[15]

The Political Argument. A third theory is that Jews are liberally inclined because that is how we express our Judaism. A core part of being Jewish, the argument goes, is following a liberal political agenda. In the 1960s, when the Jewish residents of Lakeville, a Chicago suburb, were questioned in Marshall Sklare's landmark study, they responded that "supporting humanitarian causes, aiding the underprivileged and helping blacks achieve equality were more important to being a good Jew than supporting Israel or observing the basic tenets of Judaism."[16] Another survey among Los Angeles Jews in the 1980s similarly revealed that 59% listed a commitment to social equality as the most important element of their Jewish identity.[17]

This view of social action as inherently Jewish, and for that matter inherently Democratic, comes not only from the people but also from the pulpit. Reform Rabbi Alexander Schindler wrote that the Democratic Party conveys "the ethical imperatives of the Hebrew prophets into programs to feed the hungry, heal the sick and house the homeless."[18]

Another variant of the same idea is that there are a number of issues and causes that American Jews support that, when aggregated, form the basis of a liberal agenda. However, this seems to neglect the trend toward conservatism that occurred among many Jews in the 1960s and 1970s and to ignore the preponderance of Jews who remained liberal even when the issues they cared for came into conflict with the liberal agenda. For example, when elements of the African-American community rejected Jewish support or expressed anti-Semitism, or when the political left supported the Palestinians over Israel, some Jews turned toward conservatism, while the vast majority continued to consider themselves liberal and support the Democratic Party.

[15] Shapiro 430.
[16] Shapiro 428.
[17] Shapiro 429.
[18] Edward Shapiro, "Waiting for Righty? An Interpretation of the Political Behavior of American Jews," *MICHAEL: The History of the Jews in the Diaspora*, Vol. XV (Tel Aviv: Diaspora Research Institute, 2000): 156-178.

The Sociological Argument. Sociological theories view Jewish liberalism, according to Levey, "in terms of the Jews' experience of living in close contact with a dominant non-Jewish culture. The three crucial dynamics sociologically are held to be status inconsistency, marginality and minority status." [19] This theory holds that American Jews' history of social discrimination, whether perceived or real, informs their political beliefs, as does their minority status and their identification with other minorities. However, both Levey and Shapiro dismiss this theory with equal fervor. Shapiro argues that if minority status were the key to liberalism, then the minority of Jews who are Orthodox would be the most liberal; however, the opposite is true. [20] Levey, for his part, finds that these characteristics do not explain the political behavior of American Jews. As Levey puts it: "All things considered it is hard to escape the conclusion that it is neither minority status nor a historical experience of oppression that distinguishes Jews in their pursuit of liberalism." [21]

American Jews' Attitudes Toward Judaism

Jewish attitudes toward liberalism may be best explained by their stance toward their own religion. Jews who stand in a liberal position toward orthodoxy also take a liberal position toward society. The reason for their liberalism may be how they practice their Judaism. Levey, who hails from the School of Political Science at the University of New South Wales, feels that "contrary to [the] reigning assumption that the disproportionate liberalism of American Jews has to do in some way with their relations to non-Jews and the wider society, this analysis strongly suggests that a focus on Jews' relation to their own community and religious authority is more fruitful." [22] Levey concludes: "Attitudes towards religious authority may be indicative of attitudes towards society in general." [23]

Shapiro also dismisses the widely held notion that Jewish liberal attitudes are primarily a product of Judaism or Jewish

---

[19] Levey 386.
[20] Shapiro, *MICHAEL: The History of the Jews in the Diaspora* 156-178.
[21] Levey 386.
[22] Levey 386.
[23] Levey 386.

values. As other minorities have climbed the socioeconomic ladder, they have adopted more conservative values, yet Jews continue to be identified by and to identify with liberal causes. Shapiro finds of interest that Jewish attitudes toward their own religion mirror their attitudes toward authority and hence their political stance. Shapiro finds this tension between insider and outsider, and a general distrust of authority and the dominant culture, revealed in the Jewish fiction of such American authors as Saul Bellow, Bernard Malamud and Philip Roth and in the humor of Jewish comedians such as Rodney Dangerfield, Joan Rivers, Woody Allen and Jerry Seinfeld.[24]

There is a certain logical consistency to this theory. The more Orthodox the believer, the less he stands in opposition to the tenets of his own religion, and the less he stands in opposition to the political mainstream. Similarly, the more "liberal" Jews are toward their own religion, the more they express their Judaism through their political allegiance to liberal issues. This is in marked contrast to other ethnic minorities who, as they ascend the social ladder, shift their allegiance to the status quo. As they become "American," they become loyal to protecting the established culture. Shapiro contrasts the Jewish experience with that of the Irish in America, many of whom joined the police and fire departments. The difference also can be noted in works of fiction. For example, Tom Clancy's fictional hero, Irish-American Jack Ryan, saves the Queen of England from an IRA bomb; his allegiance is to the world of law, not to the Irish.[25]

One reason suggested for this distinction is that even when American Jews climb the socioeconomic ladder and find their way into the mainstream of American culture, they retain a distrust of authority, and this remains a significant factor in their liberalism. This distrust of authority as a motivating factor can be traced to another important factor in Jewish identity: the Holocaust.[26] The Holocaust looms large as a reason why, even as Jews move from outsider to insider status, their distrust for

---

[24] Shapiro, *MICHAEL: The History of the Jews in the Diaspora* 156-178.
[25] Shapiro, *MICHAEL: The History of the Jews in the Diaspora* 156-178.
[26] Shapiro 430.

authority continues to inspire their commitment to liberal causes, regardless of their own status in society.[27] The Holocaust was a result of government-sanctioned actions that the majority never protested. The Nuremberg laws, which rendered Jews second-class citizens, were just that — laws. Although the United States did eventually enter the war and liberate the concentration camps, many Jews felt that there were elements in the government who were not so keen in aiding the Jews.[28]

The Conservative Tradition

We should not dismiss the conservative elements among American Jews. There is, in fact, a long tradition of conservatism among American Jews. *American Jewish History*, the venerable journal of the American Jewish Historical Society, devoted an entire issue to American Jewish political conservativism.[29] The issue featured a half-dozen articles, including a long historical piece by Jonathan D. Sarna, John Ehrman's essay on *Commentary* and *Public Interest,* and Midge Dector's memoir of the neoconservative movement.

Sarna's essay traces a long tradition of conservatism as fundamental to Judaism, beginning with the prophet Jeremiah, through Sir Moses Montefiore's 1864 letter to the Jewish community in Morocco.[30] Those same conservative values are present, Sarna shows, even among the colonial Jews in their earliest published liturgical composition "A Form of Prayer." [31] As the nation progressed and American Jews became part of its life, ideological conservatism did not disappear but continued to have its champions among several of America's foremost leaders, such as journalist and politician Mordechai Noah (1785-1851), philanthropist Jacob H. Schiff (1847-1920) and attorney Louis Marshall (1856-1929). This shows as Sarna puts it, that "the conservative tradition in American Jewish politics

---

[27] Shapiro 430.
[28] David S. Wyman, *The Abandonment of the Jews: America and the Holocast*, (New York: Pantheon Press, 1984).
[29] *American Jewish History* 87.2-3 (Waltham, MA: 1999).
[30] Jonathan D. Sarna, "American Jewish Political Conservatism in Historical Perspective," *American Jewish History* 87.2-3 (Waltham, MA: 1999).
[31] Sarna 87.2-3 (Waltham, MA: 1999).

does have firm historical, cultural and religious roots." [32]

George Nash, in his "Forgotten Godfathers: Premature Jewish Conservatives and the Rise of the *National Review,*" describes the journey that led seven American Jews to align themselves with the right and the role the *National Review* played in their intellectual development and careers.[33] They are William S. Schlamm (1904-1978), who helped found William F. Buckley's the *National Review*; Morrie Ryskind (1895-1985), a playwright and Hollywood screenwriter; Eugene Lyons (1898-1985), a senior editor of *Reader's Digest* and author of the anti-Communist *Assignment in Utopia*; Frank S. Meyer (1909-1972), a theoretician and editor of the *National Review*; Frank Chodorov (1887-1966), a fervent Libertarian who founded the Intercollegiate Society of Individualists as a way to combat socialism on college campuses; Ralph de Toledano (1916 -), the *National Review*'s managing editor; and Marvin Liebman, fund-raiser and proselytizer for conservative causes. Nash refers to these seven as "Godfathers" because they preceded the "neocon" era that began in the late 1960s and increased in intellectual importance (if not in actual numbers) during the Reagan era.

Conservatives Today

Although it is easy to view American Jewish voters as an aggregate of liberal sympathies whose allegiances are easily predicted, the reality is far more complicated. As Murray Friedman makes clear in his *Commentary* essay "Are American Jews Moving to the Right?": "If at the national level, Jews have predictably voted left, at the state and local level things have been more complicated and more interesting." [34]

In truth, we should recognize that the American Jewish landscape is changing, most notably at the local level. Friedman points to mayoral elections in New York and Los Angeles, where

[32] Sarna 87.2-3 (Waltham, MA: 1999).
[33] George Nash, "Forgotten Godfathers: Premature Jewish Conservatives and the Rise of the *National Review,*" *American Jewish History* 87.2-3 (Waltham, MA: 1999).
[34] Murray Friedman, "Are American Jews Moving to the Right?" *Commentary* 109.4 (2000): 50-52.

Jews have overwhelmingly supported the Republican candidate (Guiliani and Riordan, respectively). This also has been true for Governor George Pataki of New York, Christine Todd Whitman of New Jersey and Jeb Bush of Florida, who were elected with strong Jewish support.[35]

Jewish attitudes on specific issues betray a wider spectrum than the labels "liberal" or "conservative." Although liberal on issues of civil rights and sexual morality (such as being pro-choice and supporting gay rights), a 1997 AJC (American Jewish Committee) survey found that 80% of the respondents were in favor of the death penalty for people convicted of murder, and a majority seemed to be against affirmative action hiring programs for minorities or members of disadvantaged groups.[36] Friedman also cites a 1999 AJC survey in which half the respondents identify themselves as Republicans.[37] The reasons Friedman enumerates for this shift are the traditional ones: increasing affluence and upward mobility, self-interest and the fact that a generation has grown up for whom the struggles for civil rights in the 1960s are ancient history.[38] Jews may be finally becoming more like others in their socioeconomic profile. As Friedman sees it, Jews will support conservative causes or Republican candidates as long as this does not preclude or conflict with "a 'moderate' stance on such bellwether issues for Jews as immigration, abortion, gay rights and the separation of church and state."[39] This is the picture Friedman paints at the local level. As for national politics, as Friedman himself notes, every time that someone has predicted the demise of American Jewish liberalism and a shift to the right, "the prognostications have been proved wrong." [40]

The Institutional Argument

Jewish liberalism, it has also been argued, is more of an

---

[35] Friedman 50-52.
[36] Friedman 50-52.
[37] Friedman 50-52.
[38] Friedman 50-52.
[39] Friedman 50-52.
[40] Friedman 50-52.

institution than an attitude.[41]   American Jews remain liberal
because they are loyal to the idea of American Jewish liberalism:
Their parents voted that way, and they will too.[42] Another
suggestion is that, rather than being committed to liberal
policies, American Jews are loyal to the institution of the
Democratic Party. Accordingly, regardless of their views on any
given issue, Jews remain Democrats, liberal or not. Peter Y.
Medding supports this view in his work,[43] which Levey cites
extensively: "Jews are neither liberal nor conservative; they are
overwhelmingly Democrats." [44] Levey also quotes Ginsberg,
concluding: "Jews are Democrats more than they are liberals."[45]

In summary, studies confirm the overwhelming liberalism
of American Jews during the last century, not only at the
presidential level but also in local races. Jews continue to not
only be more liberal than the American population in general,
but more liberal than similar ethnic groups or similar
socioeconomic groups. The reasons for this liberalism are
complex. Attempts to explain American Jewish liberalism solely
on the basis of Judaic values and tradition, historical experience,
political benefit, the experience of marginalization or minority
status all fail. Others have suggested that a more reasonable
explanation can be traced to self-interest and a desire for
inclusion in the mainstream of American social, economic and
political life.

It is also evident that the American Jewish population is not
monolithic. There is ample evidence that Orthodox and
observant Jews are more conservative on many issues than most
other American Jews, in much the same way that evangelicals
and the so-called "religious right" are more conservative than the
majority of their Christian brethren. In addition, not only is it
possible to identify issues where Jewish groups have taken a more
conservative stance than other minorities or other groups (Israel
and the Palestinians being the most obvious example), but there

---

[41] Levey 142-143.
[42] Levey 142-143.
[43] Peter Y. Medding, "Towards a General Theory of Jewish Political Interests and Behaviour,"
    Jewish Journal of Sociology 19 (1977): 115-144.
[44] Levey 145.
[45] Levey 383.

is, in fact, a long tradition of American Jewish conservatism that
exists and flourishes to this day.

However, despite these differences, there is no doubt that
American Jews, liberal or conservative, continue to vote
Democratic in great numbers that have remained consistent for
most of the century. In this context, it is interesting to see what
impact, if any, there was when Vice President Albert Gore, Jr.,
the presidential candidate of the Democratic Party, chose as his
running mate for vice president Senator Joseph Lieberman, a
modern Orthodox Jew. During the campaign, Senator Lieberman
frequently spoke of his religious beliefs, as did both presidential
candidates. Lieberman's candidacy was an important moment for
American Jews, perhaps even more so for conservatives.
Nonetheless, American Jews voted in great numbers for Gore,
but not more than in the prior election. Was Lieberman too
Jewish or not liberal enough?

Religion: A Factor

Many political observers have commented that religion was
very much a factor in the 2000 election. This was even truer,
however, for the presidential candidates than their running mates.
It could be argued that Lieberman was selected because
presidential candidates Bush and Gore had made religion a
significant part of the campaign rhetoric. George W. Bush spoke
of Jesus as his "guiding light." [46] Gore wasted no time declaring
that he was a born-again Christian, or that when he faced a tough
decision, he asked himself, "What would Jesus do?" [47] And there
was Senator Lieberman, who, in his debut appearance with
candidate Gore on August 8th, managed to mention God a
reported 13 times in 90 seconds.[48]

Many applauded the selection of Lieberman. Gore's campaign
received a "bounce" of some 17 points in the week after the
announcement. The press attention was extensive. Many saw this
as an important moment in Jewish history. Samuel G. Freedman,

[46] Isaac Kramnick and Lawrence Moore, "Politics and Piety," *Dissent* 48.2 (2001): 4-12.
[47] Kramnick and Moore 4-12.
[48] Kramnick and Moore 4-12.

writing in *The New York Times,* said Lieberman "offered proof
that a Jew in modern America need not diminish his faith as the
price of worldly achievement...." [49]

Others wondered what the big fuss was. Commentator Ann
Coulter opined that "the way the media talk about Lieberman,
you'd think Gore had named a Martian as his running mate." [50]
She noted that, although Jews make up less than 3% of the
population, they make up 11% of the United States Senate
(including both senators from Wisconsin). [51]

As to the Lieberman candidacy being a potential source of
increased anti-Semitism, the most concerned seemed to be
assimilated Jews. Coulter chided columns by David Margolick,
William Safire and Frank Rich, who referenced increased
anti-Semitism as a potential side effect. [52] Not everyone thought
the prominence of religion in the campaign was a good thing.
There were those who felt that religion should properly be kept
out of politics. The *Washington Post*'s ombudsman reflected on
the fact that so many newspapers in trumpeting the announcement of the selection of Lieberman used the word "Jew" in the
headline. [53] She argued that this was part of the story but noted
that nonetheless this descriptive could be unfair and threatening
to Jews and other minorities who had fought hard not to be
described by their ethnicity. In a similar vein, Paul Goldman, the
former campaign manager for Governor Douglas Wilder,
writing in the *Washington Post*, opined that Gore was wrong in
asking Lieberman to join his campaign and "make history." [54]
Although Goldman felt it was appropriate for the senator to
discuss his faith as it influences his actions, it was wrong to
suggest we vote for someone just because of their religion. [55]

There were also some in the Jewish community who thought
Joseph Lieberman should have kept his religious beliefs to
himself. [56] *Newsweek* reported that when Lieberman professed to

---

[49] Samuel G. Freedman, *New York Times* 8 Aug. 2000: A27.
[50] Ann Coulter, "The Media Go Into Campaign Mode," *Human Events* 56.31 (2000): 6.
[51] Coulter 6.
[52] Coulter 6.
[53] E. R. Shipp, "The Jew Factor," *Washington Post* 20 Aug. 2000: B6.
[54] Paul Goldman, "Don't Ask Voters to Make History," *Washington Post* 11 Aug. 2000: A25.
[55] Goldman A25.
[56] Jim Wallis, "Should Joe Lieberman Keep His Faith to Himself?" *Sojourners* 29.6 (2000): 18-21.

an African-American church in Detroit that "there must be a place for faith in America's public life," he received a rebuke the next day from Abraham Foxman of the Anti-Defamation League (ADL) saying that Lieberman's appeals to belief in God ran counter to the First Amendment.[57] However, a *Newsweek* poll showed that 51% of people believe religion should play a greater role in politics.[58]

In *Public Interest*, Gertrude Himmelfarb traces the increased interest in religion to Americans' sense of experiencing a moral crisis.[59] She cites a 1998 Gallup poll that quotes 41% of those surveyed feeling that America was experiencing a "moral crisis" and 49% telling pollsters that the country was experiencing a "major moral problem."[60] This supposed crisis occurred during a time when the economy flourished, causing Himmelfarb to write: "It is this sense of moral crisis that makes Americans, even nonobservant ones, so solicitous of religion."[61]

The Public Agenda, funded by the Pew Charitable Trust, conducted the November 2000 poll "For Goodness' Sake: Why So Many Want Religion to Play a Greater Role in American Life," which suggests, "Americans have faith in faith, no matter the doctrine."[62] However, the Public Agenda also discovered that Jewish and non-religious Americans were more concerned than the rest of the population about the intertwining of religion and politics, schools and workplaces.[63]

One can argue that it was not Lieberman's Jewishness, per se, that was perceived as helpful to the Gore campaign, but rather his conservative positions. Although most Jews are perceived as hewing to a liberal agenda, the Orthodox and observant are far more conservative on certain issues (although the majority still claim allegiance to the Democratic Party). Accordingly, Lieberman was perceived as tough on Hollywood and tough on Cuba (which they hoped would be helpful in wooing Cuban-American voters in Florida).[64] In some ways, the fact that

[57] Kenneth L. Woodward, "Does God Belong on the Stump?" *Newsweek* 11 Sept. 2000: 54-56.
[58] Woodward 54-56.
[59] Gertrude Himmelfarb, "Religion in the 2000 Election," *Public Interest* 155.143 (2001): 20-26.
[60] Himmelfarb 20-26.
[61] Himmelfarb 20-26.
[62] "Most Americans See Religion's Benefits," *Society* 38.3 (2001): 38.
[63] "Most Americans See Religion's Benefits" 38.
[64] Matea Gold, "Campaign 2000" *Los Angeles Times* 24 Oct. 2000: A12.

Lieberman was religious informed his conservative opinions and made him acceptable as a candidate to Gore. Would a liberal assimilated Jew have been as attractive? Probably not to the Gore campaign.[65]

Why weren't more people concerned about Lieberman's religious stance? the *National Catholic Reporter* pointed out that, regarding how often Lieberman mentioned God, "if a conservative Christian had done that, the media would have pilloried him for breaching the wall of separation between church and state." [66] However, Martin E. Marry, in a *New York Times* Op-Ed piece, suggested an important distinction: "Nonevangelical Americans do not fear that Orthodox Jews will try to convert them, or impose their beliefs on the nation. But many people do see a threat in the efforts by evangelical Americans like Pat Robertson to change laws to conform to their beliefs and in effect produce a uniformly Christian America." [67]

After the Election

In the end, as we all know, the election was closely divided. Although the exact margin of victory is still the subject of debate, we know the following: George W. Bush is now the 43rd president of the United States, and Joseph Lieberman remains a United States senator from Connecticut.

There is some small irony that the election seemed to rise or fall on the votes in the state of Florida, a state where George W. Bush's brother was governor but for which the selection of Lieberman was hoped to have a greater impact.

According to several polls, religion did matter. One survey concluded that Bush won 61% of the votes from white evangelicals and Protestants, compared with Gore's 26%.[68] This represented a higher margin for Bush than that won by the previous Republican candidate, Bob Dole. A survey done for the Ethics and Policy Center, and co-written by John Green of the

---

[65] Coulter 6.
[66] Richard P. McBrien, "When Lieberman Talks About Faith, It's About His Faith," *National Catholic Reporter* 36.40 (2000) 23.
[67] McBrien 23.
[68] Jonathan Riskind, "Poll Shows Increasing Role Religion Is Playing in Politics," *Columbus Dispatch* 4 Feb. 2000: 3C.

University of Akron's Institute of Applied Politics, concluded that "Bush's deft handling of traditional moral issues, from abortion to presidential scandals, helped attract more white Christians" to Bush's campaign.[69]

At the same time, another survey confirmed that 77% of Jews and 76% of Hispanic Catholics voted for Gore.[70] George W. Bush did slightly better among Jews than his father, and Gore/ Lieberman did slightly worse among Jews than Clinton/Gore. Did liberal Jews alienated by Lieberman's conservative stance support Ralph Nader? Did conservative Jews side with the Republican ticket rather than the Democratic one, even though Lieberman was on the ticket? Can the Palm Beach butterfly ballot voters who voted for Pat Buchanan by mistake or whose ballots were deemed inadmissible explain the marginal difference?

It is too early to make any scholarly assessment of the election, but we can state the following: Bush still won the great majority of the religious right, and American Jews still voted overwhelmingly Democratic. But as to any further insights, we have the thoughts and opinions of at least one expert witness: Senator Lieberman himself.

On April 18, 2001, Senator Joseph Lieberman spoke on religion, politics and U.S. foreign policy at the USC Casden Institute's Third Annual Carmen and Louis Warschaw Distinguished Lecture on Jews and Politics.[71] The senator's talk was meant to complement the institute's goals of spurring dialogue about what it means to be Jewish in the West and in America. Lieberman did not shy away from talking about Campaign 2000. The senator opened his talk with some jokes about what his candidacy meant to the campaign, which bear repeating in this context not only for their entertainment value but also to show the finesse with which this experienced politician and public speaker was able to turn a politically sensitive issue to his advantage. The senator recounted that Larry

---

[69] Riskind 3C.

[70] Riskind 3C.

[71] Joseph Lieberman, address, Casden Institute's Carmen and Louis Warschaw Distinguished Lecture on Jews and Politics, University of Southern California, Los Angeles, 18 Apr. 2001.

King had suggested that Gore's selection of Lieberman as his running mate was so monumental it was like "building a bridge to the 58th century." [72] He also relayed a speech in which Al Gore had promised the Gore-Lieberman campaign would "work all out for America, 24-6." [73]

Continuing in a jovial manner, Lieberman told of the following suggested campaign slogans:

❏ "Gore-Lieberman: no bull, no pork."
❏ "With malice toward none and a little guilt for everyone."
❏ "Ask not what your country can do for you, ask what you can do for your mother." [74]

Senator Lieberman also addressed the impact that his selection had on the American people in general. The senator stated that Al Gore had indeed broken a barrier by choosing him as his running mate, and that the American people had accepted the breaking of that barrier with respect and consideration. However, the senator made clear that he felt that his candidacy did not occur in a vacuum and that he stood on the shoulders of others who had broken barriers before him: people such as John F. Kennedy and Martin Luther King, Jr. The senator stated that he experienced no anti-Semitism during the campaign, and that the campaign had not produced any greater instances of anti-Semitism in the United States. The American public seemed to have no problem with a Jewish vice presidential candidate for a major party, or with an observant candidate. [75]

Overall, American Jews voted for the more liberal of the two presidential candidates, Al Gore, and continued to vote Democratic. The addition of a Jewish vice presidential candidate did not provoke anti-Semitism, as was feared by some commentators, but demonstrated the continued success of American Jews in joining the political and social mainstream.

---

[72] Lieberman 18 Apr. 2001.
[73] Lieberman 18 Apr. 2001.
[74] Lieberman 18 Apr. 2001.
[75] Lieberman 18 Apr. 2001.

The fact that Senator Lieberman was an observant Jew may explain why he was chosen as the vice presidential candidate, in that his positions were more conservative than those of many American Jews. The fact that he was observant may explain why the senator was less likely to challenge the status quo and therefore was more acceptable as vice presidential material. This also signals a victory for the long-standing tradition of conservatism within the spectrum of American Jewish life.

Perhaps it is best to look at conservative elements within American Jewry as part of a subset within a larger group. In this context, it is easy to see how the Lieberman candidacy was an epochal event for the majority of Jews, but more so for those observant and conservative elements. We can further observe that several subsets also have been politicized. Our survey has identified several other discrete subsets of American Jewish life that have had a historically significant political impact: Jewish women in particular, Russian immigrants and the various organizations that form a large part of the American Jewish community, including the efforts of one local social service organization called NYANA. We will now turn our attention to these subsets to explore the political impact and politicization of various segments of the Jewish population.

Politics at the Institutional Level

Does the liberal bent of Jews detailed in the studies and articles quoted above carry over into the Jewish community networks of political and fund-raising institutions? Laurence A. Kotler-Berkowitz and Lawrence Sternberg took data from the 1997 National Jewish Community Public Affairs Survey to examine this question.[76] Although studies reflect that Jews tend to be more liberal than other similar ethnic groups, and more liberal than Americans are in general, they are not a totally cohesive group. Orthodox and more religiously observant Jews

---

[76] Laurence A. Kotler-Berkowitz and Lawrence Sternberg, "The Politics of American Jews: Cohesion, Division and Representation at the Instructional Level," *Jewish Political Studies Review* 12: 1-2 (2000): 160-182.

have become increasingly conservative and have dissented with other Jewish organizations on issues relating to church-state separation, abortion, homosexuality, and state recognition of non-Orthodox forms of Judaism in Israel.[77] The researchers sought to see if these same divisions played themselves out as well at the institutional level.

Kotler-Berkowitz and Sternberg found that examining the Jewish Federations, the Jewish Community Relation Council (JCRC) and synagogue members and Federation donors provided a cross section of Jews involved in political and social action.[78] Jewish Community Relation Council members were categorized as political activists and the others were divided into synagogue members and Federation donors (even though many JCRC members also belong to synagogues).[79]

Kotler-Berkowitz and Sternberg found that political activists were the most liberal. The institutionally affiliated Jews were more moderate in their political beliefs than other respondents, but they were still Democratic in their partisanship.[80] The degree of liberalism depended on the specific issue. The respondents were liberal on church-state issues, moderate on government size, had a low degree of suspicion about anti-Semitism, dovish about the Middle East peace process and supportive of religious pluralism in the Jewish State.[81] Synagogue members were the most conservative.

These results appear congruent with the theories put forward by Levey and Shapiro discussed earlier, that one's relation to one's community is an indicator of one's political leanings. Accordingly, it makes sense that there is a direct correlation between affiliation with establishment institutions and allegiance to the status quo. The more affiliated with a synagogue, the more conservative. The reverse is also true: The more one equated Judaism with social action, the more liberal one is likely to be. Those who were moderately liberal also fall under this analysis.

---

[77] Kotler-Berkowitz and Sternberg 160-182.
[78] Kotler-Berkowitz and Sternberg 160-182.
[79] Kotler-Berkowitz and Sternberg 160-182.
[80] Kotler-Berkowitz and Sternberg 160-182.
[81] Kotler-Berkowitz and Sternberg 160-182.

Kotler-Berkowitz and Sternberg stated that those who were institutionally affiliated to an organization whose agenda was social and political in nature were for the most part liberal, yet conservative on certain issues. Nonetheless, despite these distinctions, Kotler-Berkowitz and Sternberg found that in the end their similarities were greater than their divisions.

Kotler-Berkowitz and Sternberg's study concluded that there was no cause to fear that the political leanings of one group might dominate the whole process unfairly. The political divisions between the groups were for the most part erased when other variables were controlled (in some cases, a conservative position on one issue balanced a liberal position on another).[82] Although there are political divisions between the organizations and their constituencies, this does not compromise political representation within the community. On the contrary, the authors felt that such divisions may challenge leaders to evaluate their community's political interests.[83]

Jewish Women in Politics

One largely unexamined area of political activity in the American Jewish community lies within the realm of Jewish women's organizations. Historically, women have played a major role in the communal life of Jewish organizations.[84] However, too often the political contribution of Jewish women has gone unrecognized. Hasia R. Diner of New York University noted the anachronism inherent in the 1997 publication of *Jewish Women in America: An Historical Encyclopedia*, which, while otherwise erudite and extensively detailed, contained a glaring omission: There was no chapter on Jewish women in politics.[85]

The problem, as Professor Diner sees it, is that social service organizations, in which Jewish women play a major role, are not viewed as political entities.[86] The effect is that women have

---

[82] Kotler-Berkowitz and Sternberg 160-182.
[83] Kotler-Berkowitz and Sternberg 160-182.
[84] Hasia R. Diner, *A Political Tradition? American Jewish Women and the Politics of History* (New York: Oxford University Press, 2000) 21-69.
[85] Diner 21-69.
[86] Diner 21-69.

often been characterized as helpers or philanthropists, rather than acknowledging their work as political. The women are perceived as "volunteers," "club members" or "women of valor" and their efforts have been characterized as a leisure or charitable activity.[87] This ignores the strength and influence of organizations such as Hadassah, which is actually the largest Jewish organization in America. Throughout its history, Hadassah has put forward a political agenda, whether by running its own slate of candidates for the World Zionist Congress or by publicly opposing McCarthyism.[88]

Diner cites other examples of women using their "social organizations" for political action. For example, as far back as 1907 the National Council of Jewish Women was successful in lobbying a Portland, Oregon, newspaper to stop labeling Jewish apprehended criminals as Jews in their articles.[89] Faith Rogow's study of the National Council of Jewish Women, as Diner tells us, "shows how members of NCJW took stands on every major political issue of the day: social welfare, immigration policy, civil rights, nuclear disarmament, the Holocaust, anti-Semitism, Israel, McCarthyism."[90]

Jewish women may have hidden their political activity under the guise of social activity. The cost has been that the true political nature of their work has gone unrecognized. Clearly, the drive for political expression exists even within so-called charitable organizations. To see how one local agency can achieve a national platform for their agenda, we will turn to our case study of NYANA.

Local Agencies

American Jewish liberalism is not just a matter for presidential elections. It is not just an agenda expressed at meetings of the Federation. American Jewish liberalism can find profound expression through the work of a single local agency. Having examined whether the political divisions among Jewish groups

---

[87] Diner 21-69.
[88] Diner 21-69.
[89] Diner 21-69.
[90] Diner 21-69.

compromised their representation to the community, and the political role that women's organizations actually exercise, we will now turn our attention to one local Jewish agency and see what a profound effect they can have. If, as Tip O'Neill once famously remarked, "all politics is local," it is important to note the impact one local agency can have. This provides a model for local agencies throughout the nation in general, and for us in the West in particular.

NYANA is the only agency operating under Jewish auspices devoted solely to dealing with immigrants and resettlement issues. As such, they are in a unique position to comment on and contribute to a national discussion of resettlement and immigration issues. NYANA wanted to play a meaningful role in the national discussion of these issues.[91] The question was: How can a local agency achieve a national voice?

With the support of its board, NYANA decided to examine the resources available to it. Its staff members were in daily contact with its clients and had intimate knowledge of immigration and resettlement issues. Its Board of Directors was composed of committed individuals, many of whom had political or media connections. Finally, NYANA had its own clients as a potential resource: human stories that could personalize the issue of immigration.[92] NYANA realized that it could make a substantive contribution to the immigration issue. Not only did NYANA make its executives, board members and experts available to legislators for briefing on the issues, it also made them available to the media. NYANA also arranged for staff, board members and clients to testify before Congress.[93]

This gave the agency a profile and increased its credibility on these issues. Legislators and journalists came to rely on NYANA. Where possible, it used its true case histories and made its clients available to detail the human side of these issues. Particularly with regard to the former Soviet Union,

---

[91] Sandra Lief Garrett and Ellen Witman, "POLICY AND POLITICS: The Role of a Local Agency in Shaping National Public Policy," *The Journal of Jewish Communal Service* (1998): 66-75.

[92] Garrett and Witman 66-75.

[93] Garrett and Witman 66-75.

NYANA was able to access recent case histories to detail what life is like for Jews and other minorities.[94] It also identified clients whose personal experience could illustrate the effects, positive or negative, of public policy. For example, when Senator Alan Simpson, a Republican from Wisconsin, questioned whether Russian immigrants could be considered "true" refugees (given that the Soviet Union no longer existed), NYANA was able to reach out to its clients, who could detail what conditions are like in the former Soviet Union.[95] Having increased its credibility and authority, NYANA sought to expand the reach of its political efforts. NYANA approached similar agencies to unite its political efforts and increase its clout; at the same time, they trained organizations and agencies that were smaller to allow them to become advocates – increasing the potential din on any issue.[96] NYANA's efforts have been substantial in affecting legislation. For example, when there was a movement in Congress to limit the number of refugees to 50,000, NYANA worked successfully with other agencies to see that the admissions cap did not become law.[97]

NYANA is a great example of how a local agency making use of all its resources can have a national impact. As such, it presents a model for local agencies to be learned from and emulated. More important, it demonstrates how American Jewish liberalism is expressed in one local agency. Finally, we will turn our focus to one segment of the American Jewish population, new Jewish immigrants, and immigrants from the former Soviet Union in particular, and their politicization. What is remarkable is that the same drive for political action and participation is as present in new immigrants as it was in those that arrived on these shores a century ago.

The Role of New Jewish Immigrants

The role of new Jewish immigrants in American politics is

[94] Garrett and Witman 66-75.
[95] Garrett and Witman 66-75.
[96] Garrett and Witman 66-75.
[97] Garrett and Witman 66-75.

an important factor for us to consider. How have these new immigrants behaved politically, if at all? Has their experience politicized them? Do new Jewish immigrants have different values or political leanings than the majority of American Jews? Do they hew to the tradition of American Jewish liberalism or do they present a new movement to the right? We can glean some answers from the experience of Jewish immigrants from the former Soviet Union.

Soviet Jews, for example, began arriving in the United States in the early 1970s. Today, almost three decades later, they number more than half a million people.[98] In the last 30 years, there have been several waves of immigration, and the Jewish Russian population ranges from those who have raised children here to the newly arrived. Also, because of the turbulent history of the former Soviet Union, there is great diversity among the immigrants in terms of age, education, profession, fluency in English, even nationality (i.e. Georgians, Ukrainians and other members of the former Soviet Union who no longer identify themselves as Soviets or Russians).

In terms of political orientation, there has been a shift over the years in the party affiliation and voting patterns of Jewish immigrants from the former Soviet Union.[99] Many of the first émigrés admired Ronald Reagan for his strong anti-Communist stance and his willingness to stand up to the Soviet Union with increased military spending.[100] At the same time, fear of crime and concerns about lax discipline in public schools made them less liberally inclined than their American Jewish counterparts.[101] However, by 1992, most former Soviet citizens would join their American Jewish counterparts in overwhelmingly supporting Bill Clinton and the Democratic Party.[102] What changed?

One theory is that immigrants who arrived after the fall of Communism, and who had seen economic chaos ravage the former Soviet Union, were in favor of government controls for health,

---

[98] Garrett and Witman 66-75.
[99] Garrett and Witman 66-75.
[100] Garrett and Witman 66-75.
[101] Garrett and Witman 66-75.
[102] Garrett and Witman 66-75.

education, welfare and housing.[103] Also, during the early 1990s, many of the immigrants became concerned that Republicans would severely reduce programs for the elderly and other such traditionally Democratic programs as Head Start, food stamps and legal services. The threat of loss of services caused the former Soviet Jews to organize politically.[104] Significantly, although at first the former Soviet Jews allied themselves with other American Jewish organizations, they soon formed their own organizations such as the Union of Councils of Soviet Jews (UCSJ) and the American Association for Russian Jews. The politicization of the Russian community increased during the 1990s as threats to immigration levels and anti-immigrant rhetoric increased. This was particularly true in California, where then-Governor Pete Wilson supported Proposition 187, which would have prohibited health care and educational opportunities for illegal immigrants. In addition, Wisconsin Republican Senator Alan Simpson's proposed 1995 Immigration Reform Act would have made it more difficult for family members of legal immigrants to enter the United States. Russian immigrants found themselves making common cause with Latino and Asian immigrant groups to organize rallies, petitions and protests.[105]

In 1997, a series of events put into motion the most decisive political action organized by the immigrant Jewish community. President Clinton had signed the Illegal Immigration and Reform and Immigrant Responsibility Act, which increased the power of the Immigration and Naturalization Service (INS), and the Personal Responsibility and Work Opportunity Act, which affected benefits of legal immigrants who have not yet become citizens. The net effect was that there was a threatened cut of Supplemental Security Income (SSI), Medicare, food stamps and housing benefits to all immigrants who had not yet become citizens. Clinton later promised to reverse the harshest aspect of the bills, but concern grew particularly among the elderly who were at the greatest risk of losing benefits. In Los Angeles, 430,000

---

[103] Garrett and Witman 66-75.
[104] Garrett and Witman 66-75.
[105] Garrett and Witman 66-75.

legal immigrants faced the potential loss of benefits, and estimates put the number of Jewish immigrants affected at 100,000. Although one possible solution was to become a citizen (and several Jewish organizations offered crash study courses), many elderly immigrants were too anxious about their chances of passing the test. This prompted political action. On April 14, 1997, the UCSJ and American Association of Jews from the Former Soviet Union staged a protest march on Washington at which more than 10,000 Jewish émigrés protested the threatened cuts.[106] In the end, their efforts were rewarded. In August 1997, President Clinton restored cash assistance provisions for elderly immigrants as part of a balanced budget agreement. This was a watershed event for the immigrant community.

Having formed their own political organizations, Soviet Jews are now looking to work with established American Jewish fund-raising, political, social and service organizations. The Federation has established a Russian division to focus fund-raising efforts for the Russian community, and many Russian Jews are becoming involved in Jewish charitable organizations.[107] Their political engagement is part and parcel of being American.

Earlier in this chapter, it was noted that many Jews felt that a commitment to social action was central to their Jewish identity. There is no question that political action is central to Jewish communities, whether it is political associations such as NJCRAC (the National Jewish Community Relations Advisory Council), or membership in the Federation or even an affiliation with a synagogue. Concerns that political differences among these organizations might compromise their work appear unfounded. We must also recognize the contribution that Jewish women make and the political action that so-called women's organizations such as the National Council of Jewish Women or Hadassah have made throughout their history and continue to make to this day. Jewish institutions constitute an important part of American Jewish political life and it is worth noting and learning from the impact

---

[106] Garrett and Witman 66-75.
[107] Garrett and Witman 66-75.

one local agency such as NYANA can have. Finally, it is important to note how the new Jewish immigration, particularly from the former Soviet Union, has empowered itself politically. The new immigrants, much like the old immigrants, have adopted the tradition of liberalism, in that they too vote overwhelmingly Democratic.

American Jews have a long tradition of supporting the Democratic Party. This remains as true for the immigrants from the Soviet Union of a century ago, as it does for the Russian immigrants of today. This does not mean all Jews are liberal, or that all Jews who vote Democratic in national elections are liberal on all issues. Many theories have been offered to explain the phenomenon of Jewish liberalism, but we may observe that those Jews who stand in a liberal position toward Judaism tend to be more liberal on social issues than those Jews who practice their religion in a more fundamentalist or Orthodox manner. At a time when both candidates for president of the United States made their own religious beliefs part of the campaign, we should not be surprised that the vice presidential candidate is also religious. The fact that Senator Joseph Lieberman is Jewish was a history-making moment for American Jews, but more so for political conservatives and the religious Orthodox. American Jews in the 2000 election voted overwhelming Democratic, but less so than they did in 1996 for Clinton/Gore. At the same time, it is important to note that American Jews' commitment to political action is present in its Federations, women's organizations, local agencies and even among the newest immigrants. The connection between politics and American Jews continues to thrive.

Chapter Two

CULTURE:
The Jewish Role in American Arts Institutions and the Search for a Jewish Idiom

O ver the course of the last century, American Jews have had a remarkable impact on the cultural life of the United States — a role that is disproportionate to their numbers. This influence occurred not only in traditional areas such as literature or film, but also in unexpected arenas such as art museums, jazz and hip-hop. This chapter tells a tale of ethnic pride, assimilation, success and a search for what can be considered a specifically Jewish idiom. It is virtually impossible to compose a definitive survey of all the arts. As Stephen Whitfield comments in his book *In Search of American Jewish Culture*: "Readers expecting a definitive account will therefore be disappointed. For example, they may be surprised to find precious little attention given to serious or popular literature. That is because, of all the arts, it has been by far the most studied; I thus feel no need to ask anything here." [1] This is equally true concerning Hollywood filmmaking and Holocaust museums; those topics have been extensively examined elsewhere.

In this chapter, we will examine art museums, music in various forms and musical theater. In the art world, we will detail the influence of American Jewish collectors on the most prominent institutions in New York and discuss how American Jews have come to play a major role in creating the most significant modern art and cultural institutions in Los Angeles. We will also examine the roles that American Jews have played in the world of music, at both the executive level and as creative artists. As we look at the American musical theater, perhaps the most Jewish of all American arts, we will show the enduring appeal of musicals by and about Jews. As we explore these art forms and institutions, we will pay special attention to how conflicts we uncover throughout this chapter, and indeed throughout this entire survey, are manifesting themselves currently.

This chapter derives much of its material from contemporary books, magazine and newspaper articles, and other popular sources. We will apply the same conclusions about American Jewish life we have found in the chapter on politics to see if there is a consistency of behavior. Is the Jewish role in American arts to join the mainstream and gain acceptance in the lairs of the establishment? Or is there a drive to create a specifically Jewish art? In fact, both are true, and the resulting tension informs the history and recent activity we will examine in the realms of art museums, American popular music and musical theater.

Faced as they are with the homogenizing forces of popular culture, the drive of American Jewish artists to explore, create and strive for a specifically Jewish art is remarkable. The tension

---

[1] Stephen Whitfield, *In Search of American Jewish Culture* (New Hampshire: Brandeis University Press, 1999): 225.

between their achievements in works for the popular culture and
the creation of explicitly Jewish works is palpable. Yet often the
boundaries between the two blur. In Los Angeles, the Getty
Museum's expansion was led by Howard Williams, a Jewish
American, while the neighboring Skirball Cultural Center, an
institution dedicated to expressing Jewish values, does not use
the word "Jewish" in its name. Jazz legend Louis Armstrong
wore a Star of David; African-American clarinetist Don Byron
recorded an album of Mickey Katz's klezmer music, validating
the musical form for Jewish and non-Jewish audiences. Today,
the most important hip-hop executive is an Israeli-born Jew, Lyor
Cohen. Madonna's partner is Guy Oseary, who published a book
called *Jews Who Rock*. "Fiddler on the Roof" still tours and
remains relevant to Jewish and non-Jewish audiences alike.
Broadway's current hit is Mel Brook's "The Producers," winner
of a precedent-setting 12 Tony Awards, a play so ethnic we have
to ask: If it hadn't been written by someone Jewish, would it be
anti-Semitic? These are some examples of the issues
and contradictions that come up as this chapter examines the
achievements of American Jews in these three discrete arenas.

Art Museums: An Increasing Role for American Jews

American Jews have had a notable influence on the American art
scene by virtue of important roles in major American museums.
This has been true in Boston, New York and particularly in
Los Angeles. Today, many American Jews serve in important
positions in the administration, on the boards, as curators or as
important donors of American art museums. In recent years, in
New York alone, financier Ronald Perelman was president of the
Guggenheim, cosmetics tycoon Leonard Lauder was chairman
of the Whitney and his brother and fellow Estée Lauder
executive Ronald Lauder was chairman of the Museum of
Modern Art (MOMA). The recent appointment of Lisa Phillips
as director of the New Museum in New York is also significant,
as there have been relatively few Jewish women holding such
posts.

To appreciate how far Jews have come and the impact they

have made, it is important to consider the prominence over the last century of certain collectors and the impact they have had in cities such as Boston, New York and Los Angeles. Traditionally, Jews were not affiliated with the major art institutions in this country. A century ago, very few Jews held prominent positions as American museum directors.[2] As we discuss this, we will draw extensively on George M. Goodwin's two-part series published in *Modern Judaism,* "A New Jewish Elite: Curators, Directors and Benefactors of American Art Museums." The slow acceptance of Jews into the elite world of art museums in the first half of the century provides a great contrast to the contemporary scene in Los Angeles, where American Jews not only dominate the scene but played a role in establishing virtually all the major art institutions in the city, all within the last 40 years.

The First Generation

The first generation of important Jewish collectors and curators came from the American German-Jewish elite. They were, for the most part, the sons and daughters of the German Jews who founded the important merchant banking institutions and whose last names survive them to this day. Sachs, Wertheim, Warburg and Lehman are the names of American Jews who still resonate in the financial community but whose contributions to the arts are known only to insiders of the museum world.

Paul Sachs (1871-1965) was the eldest son of Samuel and Louisa Goldman Sachs. His father and uncle founded the investment-banking firm Goldman Sachs, and Paul worked there for many years after his graduation from Harvard. However, he quit banking at age 37 to become assistant director of Harvard's Fogg Museum, greatly extending the prestige of that institution during his tenure there.[3] Sachs lectured on art history at Wellesley and Harvard. As Goodwin notes: "He was one of Harvard's first Jewish professors and probably the first American-born Jew to

[2] George M. Goodwin, "A New Jewish Elite: Curators, Directors and Benefactors of American Art Museums" *Modern Judaism* vol. 18.1 (1998): 119.
[3] Goodwin 54.

teach art history in the United States." [4]   Sachs' influence
extended far beyond the Fogg. Among his protégés was Alfred
Barr, the son of a Presbyterian minister who would go on to be
the founding director of New York's Museum of Modern Art
(MOMA). Sachs himself was one of MOMA's seven
founding trustees.[5] He also strongly influenced several
important collectors, including Bernard Berenson and Maurice
Wertheim.

Bernard Berenson (1865-1959) was a famous art historian
and art adviser to the wealthy. Born Bernhard Valvrojneski in
Butrymonis, Lithuania,[6] Berenson arrived in Boston at age 10.
Although his maternal grandfather was Orthodox, his father
rebelled against religion. As a young American, Berenson was
not wedded to his Judaism. In his youth, Berenson converted to
Episcopalianism and later in life to Roman Catholicism.
Berenson, who graduated from Harvard, fell in love with Italy
and became famous as an authenticator of Renaissance art.
Through Sachs' influence he left much of his collection, as well
as his villa in Italy, to Harvard.[7] Sachs also had considerable
influence on Maurice Wertheim. The founder of the investment-
banking firm Wertheim & Company, Wertheim amassed an
impressive collection of impressionist and post-impressionist
work. Upon his widow's death, Wertheim's collection was
donated to Fogg.[8]

In New York, the Metropolitan Museum of Art was the
blue-chip art institution. Founded in 1870, the Metropolitan
entered the 20th century without any Jewish Americans gracing
its board. However, in 1909, George Blumenthal (1858-1941),
who had risen to the top of the European banking firm of Lazard
Freres, became its first Jewish trustee.[9] For many succeeding
years, Blumenthal sat alone as the only Jew on the board, among
35 members. Like Louis D. Brandeis on the Supreme Court,

[4]   Goodwin 56.
[5]   Goodwin 58.
[6]   Goodwin 52.
[7]   Goodwin 59.
[8]   Goodwin 61.
[9]   Goodwin 66.

Blumenthal was thought to hold "the Jewish seat." He guided the museum through the Depression. In 1933, Blumenthal became the Metropolitan's first Jewish president, a position he held until his death in 1941.[10] Only upon Blumenthal's death was a second Jewish trustee appointed to the Met, another well-known banker, Robert Lehman (1891-1969). This did not keep the Met from accepting many important gifts and bequests from Jewish donors, including from Blumenthal himself (he donated the courtyard of a two-story 16th century Spanish castle), Benjamin Altman (of the department store B. Altman's) and Gertrude Stein (who in 1946 donated Picasso's portrait of her).[11]

Board members exert a great influence on a museum's direction and its acquisitions, but equally important are the curators. Sachs was one of the first American Jewish art historians to wield such influence, specifically in his work at Harvard's Fogg Museum.[12] Berenson advised Isabel Gardner in assembling the collection housed in her former Boston home, now called the Gardner Museum.[13] In the Post-World War II era, Jewish curators have helped shape the way that the rest of America (and the world) views modern art. In particular, William Rubin at the Museum of Modern Art had a tremendous influence in organizing and displaying the museum's collection in a way that defined art history for that era.[14] Similarly, Henry Geldzhaler, in his position as curator of modern art at the Met, shaped the museum's collection and its image. Geldzhaler went on to serve as New York's commissioner of cultural affairs and served as patron and friend to many artists of the era such as Andy Warhol and David Hockney.[15] Similarly, in the 1980s and 1990s, Lisa Phillips worked as curator at the Whitney Museum of Modern Art, where she was instrumental in setting the tone for contemporary art by organizing the museum's biennial exhibitions of American art.[16]

---

[10] Goodwin 67.
[11] Goodwin 68.
[12] Goodwin 56.
[13] Goodwin 54.
[14] Goodwin 72.
[15] Goodwin 72.
[16] Lisa Phillips, "Bienniale," *Whitney Museum Catalogue* (New York: Whitney Museum of Art, 1992).

CULTURE 35

Despite the impressive roles American Jews have played in the life of New York's art institutions, the pace of their acceptance was slow. In contrast, Los Angeles' American Jews have actually created the major institutions for modern and contem-porary art. One could argue that no city better exemplifies the influence of American Jews on modern and contemporary art than Los Angeles.

Los Angeles: Creating Modern Institutions

For the first half of the 20th century, Los Angeles lacked any important repository for modern art. In 1910, Los Angeles County established a Museum of History, Science and Art in Exposition Park adjacent to the University of Southern California. The art department had a modest collection that remained insignificant despite gifts from J. Paul Getty and William Randolph Hearst.[17] This all changed in the 1960s, when the industrialist Norton Simon (1907-1993) was instrumental in plans to open a new and independent Los Angeles County Museum of Art (LACMA) in the mid-Wilshire area near Hancock Park, the locus of many of Los Angeles' oldest and wealthiest families.[18] Three separate buildings were planned to recognize three major donors: Howard Ahmanson, Anna Bing Arnold and Armand Hammer.[19] However, before the museum opened in 1965, Simon withdrew the majority of his support, endowing only a small sculpture terrace. Nonetheless, when it opened, LACMA was the West's largest art complex.[20]

Over the next three decades, many Jewish collectors and trustees made significant contributions to the museum. Through his contacts in the Soviet Union, Armand Hammer was able to obtain several important exhibitions. Joan Palevsky purchased an important collection of Islamic art. Phillip Berg donated his collection of tribal and ancient art. Hans Cohn gave his collection of antiquities and glass, and B. Gerald and Iris Cantor

---

[17] Goodwin 132.
[18] Goodwin 133.
[19] Goodwin 133.
[20] Goodwin 133.

presented several bronze Rodin sculptures. Among the
influential curators were several Jews, including Ebria Feinblatt,
the first curator of prints and drawings, and Maurice Tuchman,
the curator of modern art.[21] In 1974, Richard Sherwood became
president of the board of trustees and donated many important
items from his collection of Asian art. Other gifts of modern art
came from such noted Jewish collectors as David Lowe, Michael
and Dorothy Blankfort, Armand Deutch, Max and Ellen Palevsky,
Philip and Beatrice Gersh, Robert Halff, Betty Asher, Felix and
Helen Juda, Frederick and Marcia Weisman, Lucille Ellis,
Bernard Lewin and Douglas Cramer.[22] Although LACMA
established itself as a leading American art museum, it
developed a reputation as being dominated by a controlling board.
This made it hard to recruit (or for the board to select) the able,
powerful and experienced directors they needed. Throughout the
1990s, the museum seemed aimless, and there was even a three-
year period during which the museum had no director. LACMA,
it appeared, had lost its ambition to become "the Metropolitan of
the West."[23]

At the same time, several other individuals decided to start
their own museums. In 1974, Norton Simon came to the rescue
of the Pasadena Museum of Art and transformed it into the Norton
Simon Museum, a place to showcase his $100-million art
collection.[24] His collection, which focused on old masters, new
masters and Asian art, includes works by Manet, Van Gogh,
Matisse and Picasso and also boasts dozen of works by Degas.[25]
Many feel it is the jewel of the West, the "Frick Museum" of the
greater Los Angeles area. In 1979, convinced that Los Angeles
still needed a facility for contemporary art, Norton Simon's
sister Marcia, her husband Frederick Weisman (they later
divorced), and a number of prominent Jewish collectors,
including Eli Broad, the Gershes, Lenoree Greenberg, Federick
Nicholas and Max Palevsky, broke away from LACMA. Mayor

[21] Goodwin 134.
[22] Goodwin 134.
[23] Goodwin 137.
[24] Goodwin 137.
[25] Goodwin 138.

Tom Bradley then encouraged them to create their own museum as part of California Plaza, a downtown Los Angeles development project. In 1983, the Museum of Contemporary Art (MOCA) came into existence in a former police garage renovated by Frank Gehry, pending the construction of the permanent Arata Izozaki-designed building, which opened in 1986. Gehry's "Temporary Contemporary" proved so popular, it was refurbished with an additional exhibition space; in 1996, David Geffen contributed $5 million to underwrite renovation and rename the space the "Geffen Contemporary MOCA." [26] MOCA has been very successful in garnering gifts of contemporary works, including a collection of 18 American and European masterpieces from Taft and Rita Schreiber.[27]

In 1988, another Jewish collector and donor decided to found his own institution. After flirting with several institutions, Armand Hammer (1898-1990) decided that he could only donate his collection to a museum he loved, so he sought to create one named after himself. However, lacking the appropriate real estate and perhaps the time for construction (Hammer was already 90 years old), he created a facility in the building of the company he controlled, Occidental Petroleum. The Hammer Museum of Art and Cultural Center opened in November 1990, two weeks before its founder's death (and plans for his bar mitzvah). Madame Pompadour's famous saying "après moi, le deluge" ("after me, the flood") could have described the situation of the Hammer Museum after the demise of its benefactor. After Hammer's death, relatives sued and contested the will, shareholders of Occidental Petroleum complained and estate taxes and other debts were mountainous.[28] The estate was forced to sell one of its more valuable works, the Leonardo da Vinci Codex, for $30 million to Bill Gates and to merge itself with UCLA.[29] The museum continues to house Hammer's collection of prints, including his vast collection of Daumier drawings and his collection of paintings.

---

[26] Goodwin 139.
[27] Goodwin 140.
[28] Goodwin 141.
[29] Goodwin 141.

Another important cultural landmark for Los Angeles was the 1993 opening of the Simon Wiesenthal Center's Museum of Tolerance. This $50-million structure was the product of a monumental fund-raising effort by the Simon Wiesenthal Center. The board includes many of the most prominent names in entertainment and industry, including stars such as Gregory Peck and business leaders such as Samuel Belzberg and Alan Casden (who serves as co-chair of the Board of Trustees).[30] The innovative and much-praised multimedia center features interactive exhibits that teach tolerance and a Holocaust installation where visitors are led back in time to witness events of World War II. The museum receives 350,000 visitors annually, including 110,000 children.[31] What distinguishes the Museum of Tolerance from any other Holocaust museum is the reach of its ambition. The museum seeks to make activists out of visitors and to fight against hate worldwide. The museum also hosts many readings, lectures and events, and has become a dynamic and integral part of the Los Angeles cultural scene.

At the same time, American Jews in Los Angeles continued to make homes for world-class small museums and private collections. For example, Edith Wyle established the Craft and Folk Art Museum; Selma Holo is the highly regarded director of USC's Fisher Gallery, with its superb painting and sculpture collection; and Los Angeles is also home to what has been called "the most outstanding private collection of ancient Jewish coins in the world," privately owned by Alan Casden.[32]

During the 1990s, Los Angeles also saw the opening of the Skirball Center, which has greatly added to the cultural landscape of Los Angeles. Jack Skirball was a Reform rabbi for a decade before becoming the producer of such films as Hitchcock's "Shadow of a Doubt" and Claudette Colbert's "Guest Wife." He went on to have even greater success in real estate.[33] Jack and Audrey Skirball and the Skirball Foundation led the drive to

---

[30] *Simon Wiesenthal Center,* <www.wiesenthal.com>
[31] *Simon Wiesenthal Center,* <www.wiesenthal.com>
[32] Dr. Paul Rynearson, *The Numismatic Legacy of the Jews* (New York: Stack's Publications, 2000).
[33] Whitfield 225.

create a museum that showcases the "vision and values of the Jewish people." Fifteen years of planning and $90 million in fund-raising resulted in a three-story, 125,000-square-foot complex designed by Israeli born architect Moshe Sadfie located on a 15-acre site near Mulholland Drive and the San Diego Freeway.[34] Uri D. Herscher, president of the Skirball, has formulated its mission as "dedicated to exploring connections between 4,000 years of Jewish heritage and the vitality of America's democratic ideals."[35] The Skirball has a permanent collection of Judaica and has also exhibited several important exhibitions of Jewish themed art, including a special show of the work of noted artist Tobi Kahn. As part of the exhibit, Kahn exhibited a rarely seen collection of Jewish ritual objects and a series of small sculptures Kahn calls "shrines."

Nonetheless, the museum is called the "Skirball Cultural Center." The Skirball's mission is to promote a culture imbued with Jewish values. There is an extensive collection of Judaica that presents a chronological narrative of Jewish life, and although the Holocaust is discussed, the focus is elsewhere. The architecture critic Herbert Muschamp approved: "Without diminishing the meaning or the magnitude of the Holocaust, the place gathers rays of light that have penetrated through a dark century."[36] He further praised the vision of the Skirball: "Built on the idea that the power to create is stronger than the will to destroy, the display adds up to the stunning proposition that the 20th century is nothing less than a golden age of Jewish achievement."[37]

However, LACMA, MOCA, the Norton Simon and even the Skirball were all upstaged in December 1997 when the Getty Museum opened up its new six-building, $1-billion, Richard Meier-designed museum on a hilltop above Brentwood in West Los Angeles.[38] Although J. Paul Getty himself is not a name associated with Jewish causes, several Jews played an important

[34] Whitfield 225.
[35] Diane Haithman, "It's About Constructing a Cultural Legacy," Los Angeles Times 11 Feb. 2001: 57.
[36] Whitfield 227.
[37] Whitfield 227.
[38] Goodwin 142.

role in the Getty's expansion, Harold Williams in particular. Harold Williams was born in East L.A. and attended Harvard Law School. By the time he was 40, Williams was Norton Simon's protégé and served as chairman of Simon's board. He was dean of UCLA's business school before becoming chairman of the SEC under President Jimmy Carter. In 1981, he was recruited to become president of the Getty Museum.[39] In 1984, at the time of the sale of Getty Oil to Texaco, the Getty Trust had assets of $4 billion, the largest trust of any museum in the world. Williams decided to expand the Getty's mission to create several related institutes for art, education, conservation and museum management. Williams also provided grants in order to exhibit a greater percentage of the Getty's holdings. Williams retired after the Getty's opening and was succeeded by Barry Munitz, former chancellor of the California State University system. His task will be to lead the Getty into its future.[40]

In less than 40 years, Los Angeles has opened not one but half a dozen major modern art facilities, transforming the cultural landscape from a city popular for Muscle Beach and the Hollywood Walk of Stars to a serious repository of modern and contemporary art. American Jewish collectors, donors, administrators and curators have transformed the city.

We have seen the influence that American Jews have had on such cultural institutions as art museums, not only as donors or trustees but also as directors and curators. Is this struggle motivated by a desire for acceptance and participation in the mainstream of American culture? Or is this just part of the cycle of American Jews' progress through the 20th century, from minority to participation at the highest levels? (This is not unlike the journey that is charted in our chapter on politics.) We find a similar journey chronicled in the role of American Jews in the music world. In this arena, a major foundation of American society, we see American Jews both influencing the general culture and striving to create a specifically Jewish idiom that has gained appeal beyond a Jewish audience. Today there is a

[39] Goodwin 143.
[40] Goodwin 144.

veritable explosion of Jewish music of all kinds. However, as in the world of art museums, it behooves us to understand that the search for a specifically Jewish music is almost a century old and can be traced back to Romantic and Nationalistic European music movements and such forgotten composers as Joseph Achron.

A Classical Search to Create "Jewish Music"

In the world of classical music, the success of Jews as conductors of major orchestras is unparalleled. Among the giants of 20th century American music are such conductors as Maurice Avranel, Daniel Barenboim, Leonard Bernstein, Arthur Fiedler, Otto Klemperer, Erich Leinsdorf, James Levine, Eugene Ormandy, Gunther Shuller, Gerard Schwarz, Leonard Slatkin, Georg Solti, William Steinberg, George Szell, Michael Tilsen-Thomas and David Zinman.[41] There are also many classical music composers who acknowledged their Jewish heritage, including Ernest Bloch, Leonard Bernstein, Mario Castelnuovo-Tedesco and Darius Milhaud, as well as Israeli composers such as Paul Ben Haim.[42]

Several composers have also attempted to create music on specifically Jewish themes. When the Nazis came to power in 1933, Arnold Schoenberg, who was born into a German family that converted to Protestantism, converted to Judaism and decided to compose on Jewish themes.[43] His opera "Moses und Aaron" is a product of that intent.

Nonetheless, Schoenberg was composing in a non-Jewish idiom, which raises the question: How does one create Jewish music? To arrive at one possible answer, it is important to step back and view classical composition in a larger historical context.

In the mid-18th century, Europe was convulsed by several nationalist movements, which created political unrest in France, Germany, Italy and throughout the Austro-Hungarian Empire. The

---

[41] Goodwin 50.
[42] Goodwin 50.
[43] Cecil Bloom, "Joseph Achron: Maker of Music," *Midstream* 6 (1999): 6.

fires of nationalism found their way into music, as composers
like Chopin, Liszt and Brahms incorporated folk tunes into
their work. This trend continued into the early 20th century. At
the beginning of the 20th century, Jewish nationalism also was
expressing itself in the dream of a homeland in Palestine.
Concurrently, Jewish musicians began to experiment with
incorporating Jewish folk music and liturgical elements into their
compositions to create authentic Jewish music. One forgotten
composer of music with Jewish themes and melodies is Joseph
Achron. In an issue of *Midstream,* Cecil Bloom makes the case
for Achron's importance as a man ahead of his time, who sought
to define and create Jewish music.[44] Achron is significant to our
times, because we will see how a century later, we too are
witnessing the creation of music not only by artists who are
Jewish, but by artists searching to create Jewish music.

Joseph Achron was born in 1886 in Lodzeye, Lithuania. A
child prodigy, he wrote his first composition at age 7 and made
his debut at 8. He studied composition in St. Petersburg, where
he graduated with the highest honors and was recognized as a
violin virtuoso. In 1911, he joined Joel Engel's Society of Jewish
Folk Music and soon after began writing compositions using
Jewish motifs. His first creations in this genre included a violin
sonata, "Hebrew Melody," based on a theme he recalled from a
childhood visit to a Warsaw synagogue; "Chazzan," for cello and
piano; and a lullaby, "Dance Improvisation," based on the folk
song "Oi Chanukah." [45] Achron continued his explorations,
attempting to unearth the distinctly Jewish elements of
composition. Bloom believes that "Achron's main contribution
to so-called Jewish music lay in the way he handled scriptural
t'amin." [46] *T'amin* are the cantillation, the scriptural marks that
denote how a certain liturgical phrase or word should be sung.
Achron sought to adapt these rhythms and melodies to convey an
essentially Jewish sound, filled with a spiritual dimension. Achron
could use this technique on Jewish folk tunes or Chasidic

---

[44] Bloom 6.
[45] Bloom 6.
[46] Bloom 6.

melodies but also on non-Jewish melodies, giving them what Achron believed was a Jewish tone.

Achron's search to create authentic Jewish music became a passion. At one point, Achron accused two of the greatest 19th century synagogue composers Salomon Sulzer and Louis Lewandowski of being "musical anti-Semites" because they only used German/Austrian harmonization in their work.[47] Over the years, Achron composed, creating music for a Sabbath evening service as well as numerous pieces for violin and voice.[48] Over the course of his career Achron composed more than 100 pieces, over a third of which were "Jewish music, including commissions for New York's Temple Emanuel."[49] His friends liked to call him "the Chagall of music."[50] Achron traveled to Palestine and New York before settling in Los Angeles where he died in 1943. Today, he is little known and rarely performed. Cecil Bloom hopes that the time is ripe for a revival of Achron's music. He may be right. Achron was clearly ahead of his time. Keeping in mind that Achron was born in Europe and came of age in the era of musical nationalism, it may just be that it took American Jews until the end of the 20th century to catch up and develop their own nationalistic music. As we will see later in this chapter, the 1990s involve a number of musicians in the classical, contemporary and alternative music worlds in a creative explosion in Jewish music. How this music evolved from Achron's time to ours mirrors the cycle of Jewish pride, assimilation and return to Jewish roots that has been characteristic of the American Jewish population over the last century. We cannot understand the current explosion of Jewish artists and Jewish music without seeing how a prior generation climbed to the pinnacle of American acceptance.

Achron's contemporaries were more interested in joining the mainstream. This was true for American Jews as well for the great part of the century. Nowhere is this more evident than in the development of a musical form that was born at the turn of the

---

[47] Bloom 6.
[48] Bloom 6.
[49] Bloom 6.
[50] Bloom 6.

century: jazz, in general, and swing music in particular. American Jews played a great role in the creation, performance and popularization of what has been called the only uniquely American art form.

Jews and Jazz: From Creation to Mainstream Success

"[It] celebrates life – human life. The range of it. The absurdity of it. The ignorance of it. The greatness of it. The intelligence of it. The sexuality of it. The profundity of it. And it deals with it in all its…it deals with it." "It" could be the Torah, or Judaism itself, but Wynton Marsalis here is talking about the "it" that is jazz music.[51]

The first half of the 20th century saw the creation and popularization of a new musical form, jazz. Although rightly considered an African-American art form, the influence of American Jewish artists on this distinctly American music is significant. Many Jewish immigrant children found their calling playing this new music. Names like Ben Pollack, Murph Poldasky and Max Kaminsky may be lost to today's fans, but no one can imagine swing music without Jewish stars such as Benny Goodman and Artie Shaw. In the late 1930s, jazz accounted for 70% of all record sales. At that time, the most popular form of jazz was swing, and the "King of Swing" was Benny Goodman, who had his first music lessons at Chicago's Kehelah Jacob Synagogue. His great rival clarinetist was Artie Shaw (born Arthur Warshawsky). As American Jews sought to enter the mainstream of American music, they found a way to rise to the top with jazz.

Jewish Jazz

Musicologists have on occasion commented on the similarities between klezmer, Jewish dance music of Eastern Europe as played at the turn of the century, and early American jazz. Both were played by minorities on brass instruments that they had learned to play in the Army (or stolen upon deserting). Klezmer's joyous

---

[51] Geoffrey C. Ward and Ken Burns, *Jazz, a History of America's Music* (New York: Alfred A. Knopf, 2000): 40.

improvisations on clarinet and coronet were an affirmation of life, and jazz's brassy sounds were also meant to be an affront to the establishment that they mocked.

There has been extensive writing on the subject of African-American and Jewish relations. Although some critics and scholars have chosen to been critical of the Jewish role in popular culture as the stewards of movie or record companies, or to find significance in such images as Al Jolson's blackface performances,[52] our intention is different here. We wish to acknowledge the role Jews played in this uniquely American idiom and how it became an important stepping stone in the journey from outsider to mainstream participant in American culture. As for African-American and Jewish relations in the jazz world, as part of our narrative, we will pay particular attention to the formative experiences of both Louis Armstrong and Benny Goodman.

In January 2001, PBS aired Ken Burns' 10-part, 18-hour documentary on jazz. Millions viewed this extensively researched documentary. Dominating this 10-part series was Louis Armstrong, the New Orleans-born trumpet player, bandleader and singer. In Burns' estimation, Armstrong was the launching point for jazz. He was its first virtuoso and its first ambassador. Burns imbues Armstrong with an almost spiritual effect on his listeners. As publicist Phoebe Jacobs commented: "I believe — I still believe that God sent him to this Earth to be a special messenger — to make people happy." [53] Burns also makes the startling revelation that for most of his life, Louis Armstrong wore a Jewish star. The reason given in the documentary is quite moving: Louis Armstrong grew up poor in a rough and tumble part of New Orleans, where as a young child he found himself on occasions at odds with the law and in reform school. At the age of 7 and for the next four years, Louis got a part-time job before and after school driving the cart for Morris Karnofsky, a Jewish peddler.[54] According to Geoffrey Ward, Karnofsky, a

[52] Buhle and Portnoy, "Al Jolson in Black and White," *Tikkun* 11.6 (2000): 67-70.
[53] *Jazz: Part Two*, Ken Burns, PBS, Jan. 2001.
[54] Ward and Burns 40.

Russian Jewish immigrant, "collected rags and bones and old bottles and delivered coal to the prostitutes of Storyville. Louis rode in the wagon, blowing a tin horn to let clients know the Karnofskys were coming."[55] At the end of a long day, Armstrong was often invited to have dinner with the Karnofsky family. After dinner, as Mrs. Karnofsky sang lullabies to her infant son and the family joined in, Louis would be given a part to sing.

As Ward puts it: "In a world in which most of the whites he encountered were at best contemptuous, the hospitality of the Karnofsky family was a revelation."[56] Armstrong recalled: "They were warm and kind to me, which was very noticeable to me — just a kid who could use a word of kindness. Just starting out in the world."[57]

This was the first time Armstrong saw that a good family life could exist and it was where he learned many of the values that would inform his life. Not only did the Karnofsky family employ and feed him; they also encouraged him in his musical ambitions. Karnofsky lent Louis the money to buy his first cornet, which was in a pawnshop and cost five dollars. Louis paid him back from his earnings at 50 cents a week.[58] As Armstrong recalled:

The little cornet was real dirty and had turned real black. Morris (one of the Karnofsky boys) cleaned it with some brass polish and poured some oil through it.... He requested me to play a tune on it. Although I could not play a good tune, Morris applauded me just the same, which made me feel very good. As a young boy coming up, the people whom I worked for were very much concerned about my future in music. They could see that I had music in my soul. They really wanted me to be something in life. And music was it.[59]

---

[55] Ward and Burns 40.
[56] Ward and Burns 40.
[57] Ward and Burns 40.
[58] Ward and Burns 40.
[59] Ward and Burns 40.

Louis Armstrong never forgot the Karnofskys. For the rest of his life he wore a Star of David to honor their kindness and always kept matzohs in his breadbox. So we may argue that if there were no Jewish family, there would be no Louis Armstrong. No Louis, no jazz.

Having such a profound influence on Louis Armstrong would in itself mark a great contribution to jazz music. Furthermore, as Burns' documentary illustrates, over the years there has been no shortage of Jewish jazz musicians. However, if the story of American Jews in the 20th century is the story of acceptance in the highest reaches of society and enterprise, Burns makes it clear that it was a Jewish boy raised in extreme poverty in a Chicago ghetto who would make jazz the most popular music in America. This individual would take that music to Europe as the sound-track to freedom and liberation: Benny Goodman. Goodman's great contributions are acknowledged extensively by Burns in both the PBS documentary and the companion book.

Born Benjamin David Goodman in 1909, Benny was the son of David and Dora Goodman, Jewish refugees from Russian pogroms.[60] Dora, who had been working since age 8, could neither read nor write. David, who had been trained as a tailor, worked in the Chicago stockyards 12 hours a day, six days a week to support his family. Benny was the ninth of 12 children. Benny Goodman grew up in the Maxwell Street ghetto, where poverty, overcrowding and crime were rampant. For the Goodmans, there was little money and little to eat. David's only dream was that his children's education could lead them to a better life than his. He was the motivating force in Benny Goodman's life. Later in life when Benny Goodman would be interviewed, he rarely talked about his childhood, other than to praise his father. It was some-thing he preferred not to remember. Benny received his basic musical education in 1919 at the Kehelah Jacob Synagogue.[61] David Goodman had heard that a neighbor's boy was earning extra money playing in the neighborhood, so he signed Benny up in the temple's boy's band. Goodman's gift was quickly

[60] Ward and Burns 133-136.
[61] "Jazz," New Grove Dictionary of Music, 1996 ed.

apparent, and his father arranged for him to study classical clarinet privately for two years. Goodman almost immediately began playing and earning money.[62] He soon dropped out of high school and, at age 14, Goodman joined the musicians' union.[63]

Goodman's first ambition was to make money, but he was quickly recognized as a virtuoso. Goodman joined Ben Pollack's band and traveled the country with him.[64] He was a freelance musician and played in the Broadway pit for such musicals as George Gershwin's "Strike Up the Band" and "Girl Crazy" (both in 1930).[65] In 1934, Benny Goodman organized his first big band. Joining him at various times were drummer Gene Krupa, Lionel Hampton and Teddy Wilson. Early on, Goodman made it clear that race was not an issue for him. What he cared about was musicianship.[66]

"I never thought it was brave.... We just did it.... [T]hat was the way it was supposed to be. How can you play if you're gonna worry about a guy's color? It's tough enough just to *play*."[67] Over the next few years, Goodman made a series of radio broadcasts, including CBS' "The Camel Caravan." On March 3, 1937, he played a three-week engagement at New York's Paramount Theater, where huge audiences of teenagers confirmed that Goodman was the "King of Swing."[68] No Jewish performer had ever received such popular acclaim. Goodman represented the American ideals of assimilation and success in the mainstream. People didn't care about his religion; they loved his music.

Popular acclaim was not enough. On January 16, 1938, Goodman performed his legendary jazz concert at Carnegie Hall.[69] He appeared with Harry James, Ziggy Elman and Jess Stacy as well as Hampton, Krupa and Wilson from his own entourage. He also played with guest soloists from the bands of Duke Ellington and Count Basie. Jazz had reached Carnegie Hall and was finally

[62] Ward and Burns 133-136.
[63] "Jazz," *New Grove Dictionary of Music*, 1996 ed.
[64] "Jazz," *New Grove Dictionary of Music*, 1996 ed.
[65] "Jazz," *New Grove Dictionary of Music*, 1996 ed.
[66] Ward and Burns 236.
[67] Ward and Burns 240.
[68] Ward and Burns 253.
[69] Ward and Burns 257.

accepted and taken seriously. It was now the most popular music form in the United States. During World War II, Goodman was kept out of the service by a back injury but played many USO benefits and made special "V" discs for the Armed forces. In Europe, jazz was called "swing." Derided by the Nazis as "degenerate," it was taken up by Europeans as the music of resistance. At the Terezin concentration camp, the Nazis forced inmates to put on a show for the Red Cross and created the "Ghetto Swingers Band." Jazz not only grew in importance; it became the soundtrack to liberation. As quoted in Burns and Ward's book, long after the war an interviewer asked jazz great Dizzie Gillespie if jazz should be considered "serious" music. "Men have died for that music," he said. "You can't get more serious than that." [70]

Benny Goodman had proved that Jewish-born musicians could ascend to the greatest heights of popularity and musicianship. For the next several decades, Jewish musicians and singer-songwriters made their way in the American musical mainstream with little consciousness or recognition of their Jewish antecedents. As we will illustrate, many artists changed their names. Most young Americans listening to contemporary music had few Jewish idols and little reason to know if an artist was Jewish. However, the current generation of music executives and artists appear proud of their heritage and more vocal about their backgrounds.

Contemporary Music: Jewish Pride and Jewish Identity

Unlike in the art world, American Jews have played a significant role in the music business since its inception. Today there continue to be many Jewish record executives, managers, agents and attorneys who collectively have a significant impact on American music, including Clive Davis, Danny Goldberg, Mo Austin, Allan Grubman, Ken Hertz and Fred Goldring. It is particularly interesting to note how two young Jewish music executives have had a profound impact on American culture while being vocal and proud of their Jewish heritage.

---

[70] Ward and Burns 298.

No one could be more mainstream than Guy Oseary, president of Maverick Records, who balances an intense commitment and interest to Judaism with running a very successful record company and has also published a book. Oseary is Madonna's partner in Maverick Records. He not only produces her albums but also released the most successful album of the last decade: "Jagged Little Pill" by Alanis Morrisette (approximately 40 million copies sold). Born in Israel and raised in California, Oseary has always been front and center about his Judaism. He recently authored *Jews Who Rock* as an affirmation of the positive Jewish role models in the business.[71] As Oseary notes in the introduction, "I can still remember how excited I was when I learned some of my favorite musicians were Jewish – it made me feel proud of my Judaic background." [72]

Oseary's book is a celebration that lists many influential popular singers, songwriters and musical artists of the last several decades. Some are easily identified as Jews, such as Alan Freed, (the Cleveland DJ who is credited with coining the term rock 'n' roll), Bob Dylan, Leonard Cohen, Neil Diamond, Neal Sedaka and Art Garfunkel. Some are less obvious such as Courtney Love, Malcolm McClaren, Herb Alpert and Mick Jones of the Clash.[73] Of particular interest are the given names of some of today's rock stars, including:

❑ Michael Bolton, born Michael Bolotin

❑ "Mama" Cass Elliott of the Mamas and Papas, born Naomi Ellen Cohen

❑ Perry Farrell of Jane's Addiction and Porno for Pyros, born Peretz Bernstein

❑ Kenny G, born Kenneth Gorelick

❑ Carole King, born Carole Klein

❑ Manfred Mann, born Manfred Lubowitz

---

[71] Guy Oseary, *Jews Who Rock* (New York: St. Martins Press, 2001).
[72] Oseary xiii.
[73] Oseary xiii.

❏   Gene Simmons of Kiss, born Chaim Whitz
❏   Slash, born Saul Hudson.[74]

Clearly, the implication is that success in the rock world is more easily bestowed upon someone named Slash than someone named Saul Hudson. This is the contradiction inherent in Oseary's book: Although the musicians are born Jewish, most of them neither identified themselves as Jews nor made music that they or others characterized as "Jewish." These were first and foremost mainstream musicians, and no one can deny the impact artists such as Bob Dylan have had on mainstream American culture. Earlier this year when Bob Dylan celebrated his 60th birthday, the occasion was marked by the publication of several new biographies as well as a "literary panel" hosted by *The New Yorker* magazine.

Oseary's stated purpose in *Jews Who Rock* is to establish positive Jewish stereotypes and show that the landscape of popular culture is dotted with Jews. Oseary's goal, as quoted earlier, is to encourage Jewish kids listening to music to have positive feelings about their religion and heritage. To that end, he also includes the lyrics to "The Chanukah Song" by Adam Sandler. Many Jews feel left out of the popular culture at Christmas time. This is all the more true in the music world, where a long tradition of Christmas albums serves to marginalize Jews. There is some irony that it was Irving Berlin who wrote the holiday classics "White Christmas" and "Easter Parade." By contrast, could one imagine him writing a song about a Jewish holiday? As we will discuss in other chapters, particularly the education and literature chapters, until recently there was a sense that to create something that was not for the majority culture made one less of an artist, perhaps even less of an American. However, as American Jews and Jewish concepts have become more normal to the mainstream (what we might call the Bagelization of America), and with the acceptance of multiculturalism, artists feel more comfortable expressing

---

[74] Oseary xiii.

themselves as Jews, in Jewish ways. In this regard, we may look
at Adam Sandler's comic "The Chanukah Song" as a landmark
of sorts. A runaway hit, the song has now become a holiday
classic:

> *"[...]Chanukah is the festival of lights*
> *Instead of a day of presents, we have eight crazy nights*
> *[...] When you feel like the only kid in town without a*
> *Christmas tree*
> *Here's a list of people who are Jewish just like you and me*
> *[...]You don't need 'Deck the Halls' or 'Jingle Bell Rock'*
> *'Cause you can spin a dreidel with Captain Kirk or Mr. Spock*
> *– both Jewish[...]"* [75]

Oseary's book and Sandler's "Chanukah Song" can be seen
as benchmarks in a world now more comfortable with Jewish
identity. This proved true even in a world that at times has been
perceived as hostile to Jews, if not anti-Semitic: rap and hip-hop.
As president of Def Jam records, Lyor Cohen is arguably the most
important music executive in hip-hop marketing.[76] Cohen, who
was born in Israel and came to this country as a child, attended
the University of Miami, after which he returned to L.A.
Attending one of the first rap shows on the West Coast changed
Cohen's life. Soon enough, he was the road manager for the semi-
nal rap group Run-DMC. Shortly after that, he became partners
with the band's manager Russell Simmons, one of the earliest
and most successful African-American entrepreneurs, whose
more than $100-million fortune has extended beyond music, to
television and even to his own clothing line, Phat Farm.[77] Cohen's
own wealth is estimated at exceeding $40 million.[78]

Cohen's unique position in the rap world has put him in
interesting situations. For example, in the 1980s when one of his
artists, Professor Griff of Public Enemy, made a series of

[75] Oseary xiv-xv.
[76] Rich Cohen, "Little Lasky and the Big Check," *Rolling Stone* 21 June 2001: 58-61.
[77] Cohen 58-61.
[78] Cohen 58-61.

anti-Semitic statements, it was Cohen who stood by him, even under tremendous pressure. "I was the only Jew in their lives. What if I had resigned?...Instead I tried to have an impact.... I had the Holocaust Museum shut down, and we had a private tour. The first thing we see is a Jewish skull plus a black person's skull equals a baboon. The last thing is a monkey with an enormous lip, dressed with a Star of David holding a trumpet and a sign saying, 'it's these Jews that are bringing in this music called Jazz.' I believe I was instrumental in changing Public Enemy's views." [79]

Also straddling two worlds is rapper Method Man, born Ross Filler, who is part of the loose association of artists surrounding the rap group Wu Tang Clan. [80] He has recorded a Holocaust-themed song called "Never Again." [81] In a recent article, he quoted lyrics from a forthcoming song titled "Exodus": "Nowhere to run, nowhere to hide/No matter what you do to us, we'll survive." [82]

Another artist who straddles two worlds is performance artist Danny Hoch, whose "Jails, Hospitals and Hip-Hop" was presented February 24, 2001, at USC, co-sponsored by the Casden Institute. [83] Hoch was one of the first artists to bridge hip-hop and theater. Hoch produced New York's first hip-hop theater festival. In the program notes for "Jails, Hospitals and Hip-Hop," Hoch says: "Hip-hop formed my language and my entire world view. It influences my theater, whether the subject is hip-hop or not. I could be doing a piece about religion or war, and hip-hop would still inform the way I see it." [84]

Alternative Jewish Music: The Latest Trend

If Adam Sandler's "Chanukah Song" represents a milestone in American acceptance of Jewish identity, it also is part of a trend

---

[79] Cohen 58-61.
[80] Lisa Keys, "At Last: Jewish Rapper Is 'The Genuine Article,'" *Forward* [New York City] 11 May 2001:1.
[81] Keys 19.
[82] Keys 19.
[83] Danny Hoch, "Jails, Hospitals and Hip-Hop," Spectrum Series, University of Southern California, Los Angeles, 24 Feb. 2001.
[84] Hoch 24 Feb. 2001.

where artists make music about their roots. Whether we are talking about Gloria Estefan recording an album of Latin music or Aretha Franklin releasing a "gospel album," in the last decade of the 20th century artists are increasingly looking inward. At the same time, there has been a virtual explosion of self-described "Jewish music" in the United States.

The breadth and diversity of "Jewish music" is impressive. It encompasses traditional cantorial and liturgical music, Hebrew and Yiddish folk song, klezmer, avant-garde Jazz, electronica, and Moroccan and Yemenite melodies, as well as music that incorporates elements of all of the above. The start of this revolution can be traced to the reemergence of klezmer music. Klezmer, the Jewish jazz form mentioned earlier, was reintroduced to America by a group of musicians including the classical clarinetist and Soviet émigré Giora Feldman.[85] At the same time, several musicians who had been part of the 1960s and 1970s music scene, such as Andy Statman who played with David Bromberg, became observant and sought to find a way to musically express themselves in a Jewish idiom. Klezmer was the answer, and Statman was not alone.[86]

Avraham Rosenblum played for a band that opened for Jefferson Airplane in the 1960s. A decade later, while attending a Yeshiva in Jerusalem, he formed the Diaspora Yeshiva Band.[87] Yosi Piameanta started as a secular Israeli rocker. He moved to the United States and became religious, and beginning in 1994 he started to meld his rock guitar with his beliefs. *The Village Voice* has since dubbed him "The Hasidic Hendrix." [88] Klezmer bands began sprouting all over, such as the Klezmer Conservatory Band, the Klezmorim and Kapelye.[89] They played at weddings, fund-raising events and Jewish institutions and museums. They recorded albums; however, their appeal was limited, and the majority of Americans had no knowledge or appreciation of klezmer. At the same time, "Jewish music" was

---

[85] "Klezmer," *New Grove Dictionary of Music*, 1996 ed.
[86] "Klezmer," *New Grove Dictionary of Music*, 1996 ed.
[87] Alexandra Walls, "Rhythm and Jews," *Moment* 24.4 (1999): 40.
[88] Walls 40.
[89] "Klezmer," *New Grove Dictionary of Music*, 1996 ed.

in danger of becoming ghetto-ized as being limited to klezmer.

The definition of Jewish music began to expand in the 1990s due to a number of factors and events. In 1992, jazz composer and saxophonist John Zorn organized the Radical Jewish Culture Festival in Munich, Germany.[90] The very notion of holding a Jewish music festival in Germany was liberating. At the festival, Jewish musicians of every genre and style came together for a musical exploration.[91] Back in the United States, on June 1, 1993, African-American clarinetist Don Byron released a tribute album to Mickey Katz, joyously playing his klezmer trills and whoops.[92] The CD had a seismic impact, validating klezmer as an authentic musical form that can be enjoyed by the culture at large. Michael Dorff of the Knitting Factory is quoted as commenting, "[Byron] opened a lot of people's eyes. Musicians here began seeing you don't have to be Jewish to get into it, or you don't have to be religious – that this taps into your cultural roots. So then the whole *mispocheh* of downtown players all seemed to have this similar urge." [93]

In the fall of 1993, the Knitting Factory put together the Jewish Avant Garde Music tour of Europe featuring such bands as God Is My Co-Pilot, Hasidic New Wave, Gary Lucas and The New Klezmer Trio.[94] The tour visited Prague, Budapest, Germany and several other countries. At several of the stops on the tour they held discussions about Jewish issues with the public. The tour also visited the Dachau concentration camp in Germany which was described as "intense." [95] Dorff challenged the audience and artists to explore the connections between their Jewish roots and musical expression. Following their return, the Knitting Factory began to host Jewish music festivals, including Jewsapalooza (named after the popular alternative music festival Lollapalooza). The Knitting Factory also began to host Passover Seders, which by 1998, its third year, attracted more than 700

[90] Walls 40.
[91] Walls 40-47.
[92] Walls 40-47.
[93] Walls 40-47.
[94] Walls 40-47.
[95] Walls 40-47.

attendees and some 6,000 online participants.[96] More recently, the Knitting Factory has opened a branch in Los Angeles that hosts a regular Sunday "Klezmer Brunch" (a contrast to the House of Blues "Gospel Brunch"), a website devoted to Jewish alternative music called "oyhoo" (www.oyhoo.com) and a record label called JAM.[97]

Dorff's efforts helped broaden the American definition of popular music, allowing artists to experiment with Jewish forms for a much wider audience. When the New Orleans Klezmer Orchestra plays dates at the New Orleans Jazz and Heritage Festival, the crowd is standing room only. Today, in any record store one can find recordings of "Jewish music" in every section from jazz to alternative to world music. Among the artists extending the definition of "Jewish music" are the New York group Pharaoh's Daughter, Los Angeles-based Bruce Burger (known professionally as Rebbe Soul) and jazz artist Uri Caine.[98] Caine is equally comfortable in the worlds of classical music and jazz, and his works have often blended the two, most notably in his improvisations on Bach's Goldberg Variations.[99] In the world of Jewish music he is a regular at the Knitting Factory and has collaborated with Ari Benoussian, a Moroccan-born cantor, to record a CD inspired by the Zohar.[100] Today, Jewish music is rich, vibrant and diverse.

At the end of the last century a nationalist movement in music led some artists to explore Jewish music in the classical idiom. Among these artists, Joseph Achron is nearly forgotten and deserving of revival. Achron attempted to isolate the specifically Jewish melodic elements found in the cantillation of prayers and to create a vocabulary for composition that was authentic. His contemporaries preferred to work in the popular idioms of the day even when composing music for synagogues. One can barely imagine 20th century classical conducting and composition without the contributions of American Jews such as

---

[96] Walls 40-47.
[97] *JAM* <www.oyhoo.com>
[98] *JAM* <www.oyhoo.com>
[99] Ted Panken, "Non-Categorical Variations," *Down Beat* 68.6 (2001): 40-45.
[100] Panken 40-45.

Leonard Bernstein and Michael Tilson-Thomas.

As the century progressed, American Jews assimilated into the dominant culture in an unprecedented fashion. This was particularly true in the first half of the century in that most American of musical forms, jazz. At one time the most popular music in America was jazz, and the most popular musician in America was the "King of Swing" Benny Goodman, the child of Russian Jewish immigrants, raised in Chicago's Market Street ghetto. Goodman cared more about musicianship than race or religion and America accepted and revered him for his virtuosity.

As we entered the second half of the 20th century, Jews had so successfully assimilated into American music that there was no real Jewish identity in their music. This led many contemporary rock artists to change their names while achieving great success in the mainstream culture. Nonetheless, American Jews continued to exert great influence in the music industry. Madonna's partner in her recording company is Guy Oseary. One of today's most successful hip-hop executives is Lyor Cohen of Def Jam, who is especially notable in the ways he influences his recording artists. Among the influential Jewish rap and hip-hop artists are Method Man and Danny Hoch.

As the 20th century came to a close, certain artists began exploring Jewish music and making Jewishness part of the musical landscape. Among the landmarks we can look to is Don Byron's tribute to Mickey Katz in 1993, the Knitting Factory's festival of Jewish Alternative Music and Adam Sandler's surprisingly popular comic holiday classic, "The Chanukah Song."

The American Musical Theater:
From Sholem Aleichem to Mel Brooks

As great as the influence of American Jews is on popular music, one can't even conceive of American musical theater without George and Ira Gershwin, Rodgers and Hammerstein, Abe Burrows and Stephen Sondheim, to name just a few. Actor and cultural icon Marlon Brando has stated: "If it weren't for the Jews we wouldn't have much theater. We wouldn't have, oddly enough, Broadway and Tin Pan Alley and all the standards that were written by Jews, all the songs that you love to sing."[101] However, even in the musical theater American Jews have balanced making works that assimilate them into the mainstream with works that are clearly identified as Jewish. In this sense, we can see the same trends in musical theater as we have already discussed in reference to art museums and music.

As mentioned above, the Jewish role in American theater in general and in musical theater in particular is perhaps greater than in any other art. This is true historically and even more so today. The greatest theater phenomenon of recent memory is the current record-setting box office smash — Mel Brooks' "The Producers." Twelve Tonys, 18 nominations, $100 ticket prices, and sold out months in advance — all for a play within a play called "Springtime for Hitler." Contemporaneously, "Fiddler on the Roof," another Broadway musical stalwart, equally Jewish in theme and characters, continues to be performed. What is the enduring appeal of "Fiddler" for Jews and non-Jews alike, and what does it tell us about the Jewish role in American life? What does it tell us that Tevye continues to fiddle, while Max Byalistock fiddles with the books for his play? How we reconcile these two? At the same time, our survey has uncovered a drama playing itself out in the most purely Jewish of American theater traditions, the Yiddish theater. The tensions that characterize the Jewish community as a whole are played out in this dispute, which claims to be about the soul of the Yiddish theater.

Yiddish Theater: A Fight in the Family

The Torah tells us that the night before he was to reunite and reconcile with his brother Esau, Jacob wrestled with God. It seems that since then Jews have always been arguing with each other.

There is the old Jewish joke about the man who was marooned for many years on a desert island. When he was finally rescued, the man took his rescuers on a tour of the island. "This is the house I built, and this the garden I planted. Here is the greenhouse and here the pen for animals. Over here is the

---

[101] Whitfield xii.

synagogue. And over there is the other synagogue."

"Two synagogues? Why?" the visitor asked.

"No one goes to that one."

Even in the Yiddish theater, an art form that needs all the strength and unity it can get, a fight has broken out.[102] In 1998, the Folksbeine Theater (the People's Stage), the longest continuously performing Yiddish theatrical institution in the world, decided to bring in younger talent, naming Zalmen Mlotek and Eleanor Raissa (in their 40s) as co-artistic directors. In response, the Folksbiene's matriarch Zypora Spaisman, who had been at the Folksbiene for more than 50 years, took the theater's mailing list with her. She promptly created her own institution, the Yiddish Public Theater. The net effect for the public is wonderful: There are now two Yiddish theaters in New York. But the differing philosophies of the two companies are illustrative of the trends and rifts in Jewish theater.

The Folksbiene was founded in 1915 on the Lower East Side of Manhattan[103], one of 14 professional Yiddish theaters. The Folksbiene formed an alliance with the Workmen's Circle, developed a repertory of original and adapted plays, and became one of New York's leading Yiddish theater companies.[104] However, through the 1920s, '30s, '40s and '50s, the audience declined steadily. By 1956, there were few Yiddish speakers and the audience was aging. Enter Zypora Spaisman, who emigrated from Poland where she had been an amateur actor and supported herself as a midwife.[105] In New York, Spaisman auditioned and won a role in a Folksbiene production. She continued to play roles and support the theater, selling tickets and eventually joining the board.[106]

Zalmen Mlotek's father was the cultural director of the Workmen's Circle, his mother writes a Jewish music column for *The Yiddish Forward,* and he grew up breathing Yiddishkeit. He

[102] Nahma Sandrow, "A Real Life Family Drama in the Yiddish Theater," *New York Times* 24 Dec. 2000: 2.
[103] Sandrow 2.
[104] Sandrow 2.
[105] Sandrow 2.
[106] Sandrow 2.

is on the faculty of Yeshiva University's School of Music and directs the Lincoln Center Summer Klezmer All-Star Concert. With his cousin Moshe Rosenfeld, Mlotek has created the popular Yiddish-English revues "The Golden Land" (1985) and "Those Were the Days" (1990).[107] Eleanor Raissa, the child of Holocaust survivors, grew up in a Yiddish-speaking home in Brooklyn and was headed for a career on Broadway when she answered the casting call for the chorus of a Yiddish musical. As happened in the Hollywood legends of old, the star became ill, she filled in, and a star was born.[108]

While performing at the Berlin Festival of Jewish song in 1997, Mlotek and Raissa got the idea of transforming the Folksbiene into a theater that would capitalize on the resurgence of Yiddish arts.[109] Mlotek and Raissa wanted to draw in younger audiences, even ones that do not speak Yiddish. This provoked deep conflict with Spaisman, who wanted to hew to classic, all-Yiddish productions.

Here we have the quintessential dilemma affecting American Jews in the 21st century. Given that America has come to accept, even embrace, so many elements of Jewish culture, do we create new hybrid forms that can be enjoyed by a greater number of American Jews and by non-Jews? Or are we secure enough in our position in American society that we should avoid compromise but instead revive the classics for a new generation? Clearly, the ideal answer is that we should do both, but whether one of these competing factions will gain supremacy over the other is unclear.   In any event, it is an indication of where we stand in American culture that both are being pursued.

Now Playing: "Fiddler" and "The Producers"

This same conflict is being played out in the popular theater as well. It is interesting to note that at the same time that "The Producers" is all the rage, the old chestnut "Fiddler on the Roof," the musical based on the stories of Sholom Aleichem, continues

---

[107] Sandrow 2.
[108] Sandrow 2.
[109] Sandrow 2.

to tour. A recent production in Washington, D.C., starring Theodore Bikel as Tevye, received warm reviews and demonstrates the enduring appeal of this story.[110] Its ability to charm successive generations of Jews and non-Jews alike lies in the dilemma that Tevye faces: how to remain Jewish and maintain traditions in a modern world beset by assimilation and revolution.

"Fiddler" straddles both worlds. The play's Jewish references are specific, but the attitude is sentimental, bordering on schmaltzy. This is true for the music, lyrics and choreography as well. Songs such as "Sunrise, Sunset," "Tradition" and "If I Were a Rich Man" are sentimental, yet they make wonderful use of Jewish folk melodies (Achron might even approve). Similarly, Jerome Robbins' choreography is inspired by and borrowed from Jewish dance. As one critic noted, Fiddler's "mix of Jewish culture with universal human concerns continues to speak — indeed, sing — to the present."[111] However, it is Tevye's struggles with his children that make the play remain relevant and acceptable. The message of this story is: be conscious of your roots, appreciate them, and go into the future. In essence, Tevye accommodates the outside world. In contrast, "The Producers" can only be described as a work of chutzpah. Its success lies in the unapologetic tone with which it revels in crass Jewish stereotypes.

"The Producers" is a phenomenal success, winning an unprecedented 12 Tony awards out of a record 18 nominations. Rarely has such an overtly Jewish figure as Mel Brooks dominated the Tonys. Born Melvin Kaminsky in Brooklyn on 1926, Mel Brooks wrote for Sid Caesar, and together with Carl Reiner he developed his "2000 Year Old Man" routine. His movies such as "Blazing Saddles," "Young Frankenstein" and "History of the World, Part One" made him an extraordinary comic force for decades in Hollywood. According to Steven Suskin's "Opening Night on Broadway," Brooks' idea for "The Producers" had its genesis in the 1962 Charles Strouse-Lee Adams musical "All American," for which Brooks wrote the book.

---

[110] William Triplett, "For 'Fiddler,' Another Sunrise" *Washington Post* 7 Jun 2001: C1.
[111] Triplett C1.

Despite high expectations — Strouse and Adams had created the hugely successful "Bye Bye Birdie" — "All American" closed after just 80 performances, a tremendous failure for the time. Brooks, Suskin wrote, wondered: What would happen if someone tried to intentionally produce a bad musical?[112]

From that germ of an idea, the film "The Producers" was born. The plot involved Max Byalistock, an impoverished Broadway producer who makes his living by romancing old ladies. Byalistock convinces his accountant Leo Bloom to over-finance a sure-to-fail play, "Springtime for Hitler," so that they can take the money and run to South America. The supporting characters include Franz Liebkind, the ex-Nazi author of the play "Springtime for Hitler," the director Roger DeBris (that's the joke: the bris), and the play's star, Lorenzo St. Dubois, whose friends call him LSD, and who plays Hitler for laughs. There are madcap musical numbers with goose-stepping Nazis. Despite Byalistock and Bloom's plan, the play becomes a surprise hit, thereby ruining the two, who, desperate, decide to blow up their building. In the end, they are trapped in the explosion and caught by the police. The film was released in 1968.

Life imitates art: "The Producers" was a movie that the studios thought was sure to fail. They kept it on the shelf unreleased until Peter Sellers stumbled onto a print, screened it, and declared it to be the funniest movie he had ever seen. The movie did not fare well at the box office but won Mel Brooks a screenwriting Oscar. It took almost 40 years for the movie to become a musical. It is ironic that by the millennium many in Hollywood were ready to write off Mel Brooks. He had not had a hit in many years, and his last several movies were not well received by critics or by the public. The problem was that Mel Brooks kept putting musical numbers in his films, and no one was interested in musicals. Musical comedies, it was thought, were dead. Although Brooks was considered funny, no one thought of him as a songwriting talent. Enter David Geffen, who hectored Brooks into believing it could be a musical and stepped

---

[112] Steven Suskin, *Opening Night on Broadway* (New York: Music Sales Ltd., 1990).

aside for a host of other producers to come aboard. Brooks wrote more than 20 songs for the musical; the rest is Tony history.

But what does "The Producers" teach us about the Jewish role in American life? If there is any lesson, it is that there is no longer a subject that is "too Jewish" and that it is okay to have negative stereotypes of Jews if: a) the story is a comedy; b) other ethnicities are insulted as well; and c) the writer is Mel Brooks. What is clear is that "The Producers" succeeded as a Broadway musical, and probably would not have been written in the first place, 50 years ago, in the era of Benny Goodman and George Gershwin.

Over the last century, American Jews have made tremendous contributions to the arts, sometimes in unexpected ways. They have emerged as significant collectors, donors and directors at many of the country's most important art museums, including Boston's Fogg Museum and New York's Metropolitan Museum of Art. At one time in New York, prominent American Jews sat at the heads of the boards of the Museum of Modern Art, the Guggenheim Museum and the Whitney Museum of American Art. Forty years ago, Los Angeles was barren of significant museums or facilities to show modern art. Today, partly because of the efforts of a small group of local Jewish collectors and museum officials, there are more than half a dozen major institutions in the greater Los Angeles area, such as LACMA, the Norton Simon Museum, MOCA, the Hammer/UCLA Museum, the Museum of Tolerance, the Skirball Cultural Center and the Getty Museum.

In the world of music, American Jews have reached unparalleled levels of fame and achievement. They have contributed important conductors and composers to classical music. In the 1930s, Benny Goodman helped jazz become the most popular music in the country. In the rock era, beginning in the late 1950s and continuing until the present, Jewish singers, songwriters and musicians were absorbed by the popular culture, even as they changed their names to do so. American Jews continue to play important roles as executives and artists, but there is a new generation that is more vocal about their heritage. These include Guy Oseary at Maverick Records and Lyor Cohen at Def Jam, as well as artists such as Method Man, Danny Hoch and Adam Sandler, whose comic "The Chanukah Song" became an instant classic. At the same time, it has taken American Jews almost a century to catch up with Joseph Achron, the Lithuanian-born composer who sought to create a specifically Jewish idiom in composition, and who is deserving of a revival. Today a number of artists are engaged in a vital exploration of Jewish music in a variety of forms, and Jewish alternative music draws record crowds of Jews and non-Jews all over the country and all over the world.

Finally, in the world of musical theater, possibly the most Jewish of all American art forms, two musicals, both with Jewish characteristics, but with very different attitudes, are currently being performed: "Fiddler on the Roof" and "The Producers." One is sentimental about its Jewish context, the other is brazen; both delight audiences of Jews and non-Jews alike.

We may conclude that at the beginning of the 21st century, American Jews have achieved the highest levels of acceptance and success from cultural institutions and, as artists, from the rest of the culture by virtue of their talent. They have no need to hide their heritage and are freer than ever not just to use and explore Jewish themes, but to disregard them if they choose.

Chapter Three

VALUES:
New Organizations and New Initiatives in Philanthropy

In this chapter we turn our attention to Jewish values, focusing on the evolution of one value in particular, charitable giving, and its role in Jewish American life today. Philanthropy has essentially become the backbone of the world's nonprofit and research organizations; institutes such as ours would not exist without the community's generosity. It is, therefore, critical that the philanthropic community of organizations and individuals also stay informed about the work that is being done, where and by whom, and the perception, needs and desires of the work's recipients. We will begin with a brief overview of the Jewish tenets that inform the fundamental principles of the Jewish philanthropic tradition. With that in mind, we will then review the organizations, participants and money affecting the national and international Jewish communities. We will also take a look at some areas of conflict, the mission and the challenges facing Jewish philanthropy at the beginning of the 21st century.

Let us begin our inquiry with a deliberately provocative question: Why philanthropy? Or to put it another way: In examining the Jewish role in American life, why are American Jews so charitable?

American Jews represent only a small percentage of the population; however, we play a major role in the health-care related charities and cultural institutions in the United States. In the world of American art museums, as we discuss at greater length in the chapter on Culture, Jewish participation as donors, board members and directors is extensive, particularly in New York. In Los Angeles, American Jews have been critical in creating almost all the major modern art facilities.

Why be charitable? The reason most often given is that charity is integral to most American Jews' notions of Judaism. In this chapter, we will not only discuss why Jews are charitable, but also what occurs once they decide to be charitable. There is a tension between the individual act of generosity and the act of the community making decisions as a group.

Tradition of Giving

The Hebrew word *tzedakah,* meaning charity and righteousness, is a central concept in the Jewish tradition. Numerous references to charitable behavior can be found in the Torah (Deuteronomy, Leviticus, Exodus), the Talmud and in the collective memory of secular Jews who recall the *pushke* or "blue box" of their childhood homes. According to David G. Dalin, the biblical concept of *tzedakah* and its fundamental principles of self-help and communal self-sufficiency have been the essence of the Jewish view of charity and philanthropy from biblical Israel through much of modern American life.[1] Relating to the principle of self-help, Dalin writes that the purpose of *tzedakah,*

---

[1] David G. Dalin, "Judaism's War on Poverty," *Policy Review* 85 (1997): 28-33.

according to the rabbis of the Talmud, is to help others help themselves.

One of the interesting areas in which this dynamic presents itself in contemporary society is with regard to the issue of welfare. Historically, Jewish society has not condoned existing on welfare, and has instead exerted tremendous religious and political influence by recognizing that the stigma of dependency may lead to shame. Lending, rather than giving, is the far more meritorious form of charity in the long run.[2]

Nonetheless, the terms of Jewish settlement in America, that Jews were required to "take care of their own," reinforced the biblical idea of self-sufficiency. Further, the concept of "taking care of their own" laid the groundwork for the network of philanthropic and community organizations that would come to support the arrival of new immigrants from the 17th century through the 1990s.[3]

Tzedakah is part and parcel of another core value in the Jewish tradition, the obligation to repair the world or *tikkun olam*. The *Aleinu* prayer that ends every Jewish service mentions that this action on the part of the Jewish people is what will accompany the ultimate establishment of God's kingdom on Earth. Programs that address broader social issues, such as shelters for battered women and anti-poverty programs, are often considered to exemplify this precept, expressing their founders' Jewish identity by bringing the Jewish imperative for social justice explicitly into the philanthropic world.

The Jewish Fund for Justice (JFJ) is just one example of the many public grant-making foundations providing support to some non-Jewish assistance programs, whose leaders cite *tikkun olam* as the basis of their work. When confronted with questions or opposition to their mission, Marlene Provizer, executive director, simply answers, "The concept of *tikkun olam* implies that each of us is compelled not to passively accept the world's imperfections, but to try to do something about them here on Earth." To her, the activities of the organization come directly

---

[2]   Dalin 28-33.
[3]   Dalin 28-33.

from her Jewish values.[4] And these broad-based foundations are not alone.

Jeffrey Solomon invokes these concepts in his paper on reinventing Jewish communal structures. Referring to *tzedakah* and *tikkun olam,* he writes, "The success of the system is predicated on core Jewish values that speak to the infinite value of humankind, our responsibility to one another, our responsibility to heal the world, and our responsibility to care."[5]

The remainder of this chapter updates the contemporary situation in American Jewish philanthropy, what has come to be a world of its own, based in part on the precedents set by these biblical traditions.

As the desire to be charitable plays itself out in an organization, inevitable conflicts arise — tensions between individual goals and group goals. Also, as the culture changes, so too do the patterns of philanthropy. In prior generations, anonymous giving was upheld as a standard to be envied. Today, many donors are more comfortable with recognition for their actions and seek targeted goals for their giving. These tensions have played themselves out within the Jewish philanthropic community, which has attempted to refashion itself to be more responsive to its members and to its times. At the same time, there continue to be individuals who go their own way, making contributions that are innovative and substantive. We will examine both the traditional and newer institutions to see how philanthropy plays itself out at the organizational level.

The Merger

In November 1999, following more than five years of oftentimes contentious negotiations,[6] the United Jewish Appeal (UJA), the Council of Jewish Federations (CJF) and the United Israel Appeal (UIA) merged to become the United Jewish

[4] Jonathan Groner, "Funding Social Change: Jews, Philanthropy & Justice," *Jewish Funders Network Quarterly Newsletter,* Spring (2000): found through *Jewish Funders* website <www.jfunders.org>, and page references are according to web pagination: 1-4.
[5] Jeffrey R. Solomon, "Reinventing Jewish Communal Structures: The Creation of the United Jewish Communities," *Journal of Jewish Communal Service* 76 (1999): 68.
[6] Lawrence Grossman, "The Organizational World," *American Jewish Yearbook* (2000): 239.

Communities (UJC), an umbrella organization hoping to
collect and redistribute a large percentage of North America's
philanthropic dollars. The reverberations from this colossal union
continue to be felt today as the "united" community organization
struggles to simultaneously identify the priorities of its
constituents and refine its definition of self. To be sure this is no
small feat, given the different tenor and goals of the predecessor
organizations.[7]

Imagine the Microsoft and Apple computer corporations,
longtime competitors in the personal computer market, deciding
to pool their resources and develop a universal operating system.
The new system must have all the latest bells and whistles
necessary to attract the young and savvy new consumers, while
maintaining enough of the old, individual system identities to keep
their more traditional customers' loyalty. The new system must
do this while ensuring that no business is lost, all processes
remain functional during the transition and while carefully
positioning itself to lead users through the next generation.

This is the task facing the leadership of the newly formed
UJC. Part of the difficult transition process was selecting the right
leaders. In February 1999, Charles Bronfman won unanimous
approval of the 25-person nominating committee to serve as
chairman of the board.[8] According to Reed Abelson of the *New
York Times*, even before the merger was officially finalized, the
choice of Bronfman was an effort to bridge the gap between the
critics and champions of the prior directors.[9] Known for both his
strong ties to Israel and for having been active in the groups
without being a member of the former leadership, Bronfman
describes himself in the same article as "an encourager of
change," stating, "I think there is a great opportunity for rebirth,
rethinking."[10]

The subsequent leadership decisions proved more challenging. Several months later, now president and chief executive

[7] Solomon 64.
[8] Grossman 239.
[9] Reed Abelson, "Merger Near, 2 Jewish Philanthropy Groups Pick a Leader," *New York Times*
14 Feb. 1999, late ed.: 20.
[10] Abelson 20.

officer Stephen Solender was initially appointed as part-time interim president for six months, while giving the consensus-less search committee more time to make a recommendation for the position.[11] Later still, Louise Stoll, a Clinton administration and private industry manager,[12] was chosen as executive vice president and chief operating officer, and David Altshuler, founding director of the Museum of Jewish Heritage in New York, was selected to head one of the biggest new initiatives, a semi-autonomous trust fund designed to reconnect with large donors by enabling them to pursue specific projects of interest.[13]

The UJC needed to address the criticisms of the old organizations. According to the *New York Times*, the UJA and Jewish Federations had come to be regarded as "unresponsive to donors and uncreative in their giving," inciting several major donors to redirect their dollars toward other causes or to establish and contribute through personal foundations over which they had more direct control.[14]

Jack Wertheimer, professor and provost at the Jewish Theological Seminary, has found that donors of the baby-boom generation have more desire than their parents to know "exactly what their money is going toward." A participant in the year 2000 "Reappearing American Jew: Identity and Continuity" conference co-sponsored by the USC Casden Institute, Wertheimer states the baby-boomer's interest lies in helping a particular cause or place and that "this is a pattern in philanthropy across the board."[15]

Gary Tobin also identifies several patterns in philanthropy, noting that people who give out of a sense of communal responsibility are not necessarily acting for religious reasons, that givers tend to have stronger Jewish friendship networks than non-givers and that younger Jews are less likely to give because

---

[11] Grossman 239.

[12] Grossman 240.

[13] Lisa Miller, "Can a Venerable Jewish Charity Make a Comeback? The UJC's Aim to Rekindle Concern for Global Judaism Is Plagued by Infighting," *Wall Street Journal* 19 Jan 2000, eastern ed.: B1.

[14] Abelson 20.

[15] Associated Press, "Merger Reflects New Strings Tied to Donations; Charity: New Patterns of Giving Are Forcing Fund-Raisers to Adapt. Donors Want More Personal Stakes in Their Benevolence," *Los Angeles Times* 27 Nov. 1999, valley ed.: A13.

they are less involved.[16]

Robert Levitan, founder of iVillage, Inc., is one who exemplifies these changing patterns. With major money to give for the first time, he stated his choice to support Makor, a Jewish singles club, rather than make a contribution to the UJC was based on his preference to support "things I'm familiar with and people I know." [17]

Alan Casden also subscribes to this changing approach to giving. The endowment of the Casden Institute for the Study of the Jewish Role in American Life, his service to the International Committee for the Jerusalem 3000 celebration, his input toward the creation of the Museum of Tolerance in Los Angeles in 1993 and his participation with numerous boards of Jewish organizations, all support Casden's long-maintained personal interest in the role that Jews play in their communities and in American and world society.[18]

Even Charles and Andrea Bronfman themselves are involved in personalized giving. Together with Michael Steinhardt, they helped launch the Birthright Israel program, which underwrites student trips to Israel.[19] That even such traditional organizational donors feel compelled to create new initiatives is striking and meaningful. This new pattern is at odds with the central collection and disbursement model of the prior, separate philanthropic entities and will have to be dealt with by the governing bodies of the UJC and by those Federations who were not quick enough to readjust their allocation mechanisms to reflect these trends.[20]

The Federations were also criticized for their outmoded focus. The Federations were created to provide social services for refugees a century ago, and the UJA was established to rescue Jews from Nazi Europe. Many felt they had failed to act quickly enough to recognize the shift in the donors' priorities.

---

[16] Gary Tobin and Adam S. Tobin, "American Jewish Philanthropy in the 1990s," *Cohen Center for Modern Jewish Studies* (1995): 1.

[17] Miller B1.

[18] Alfred Kidlow, "Trustee Alan Casden Gives $10.6 Million," *USC Chronicle* 13 Nov. 2000: 1-2.

[19] Associated Press A13.

[20] Solomon 64.

J.J. Goldberg tells us the emergency today is that young Jews no longer wonder whether they will survive but, instead, wondering, "why [to] stay Jewish in a world that's ever more welcoming." [21] Tobin suggests that while "supporting Israel and social welfare causes, helping Jews in crisis, fighting anti-Semitism, upholding causes of social justice and strengthening the Jewish community remain significant motivations for giving," Jewish organizations would do well to stress "community building" themes in their fund-raising efforts and to provide "hands-on" learning experiences that link campaign drives to concrete programs. [22]

Born of an effort to address these criticisms, the merger created new problems for the United Jewish Communities. The proposed distribution of power within the policymaking bodies of UJC, emphasizing Federation "ownership," alienated the religious bodies, rabbinical organizations and Zionist groups that represent a portion of the broader Jewish community. [23] Even among Federations, divisions emerged. One side, led by Barry Shrage of the Combined Jewish Philanthropies of Greater Boston, is espousing the "need to create our own identity" and de-emphasizing giving to Israel. [24] Robert Aronson of Detroit's Federation summarizes the opposing argument, the one endorsed by UJC headquarters, stating, "There has to be a sense of commitment and obligation and responsibility to Jews [...] who aren't living next door." [25]

So where does UJC stand today? In 1998, the UJA membership dreamed of a visionary organization that would provide a resource for young families and a magnet for the dollars of affluent Jews. [26] The original mission statement proposed to continue the traditional role of supporting projects in Israel and overseas and supplementing that with programs that foster Jewish renaissance and renewal at home. [27] In order to

---

[21] J.J. Goldberg, "Jewish Philanthropy, From A to C," *The Jerusalem Post* 29 Nov. 1999: 6.
[22] Tobin 1.
[23] Grossman 239-240.
[24] Miller B1.
[25] Miller B1.
[26] Miller B1.
[27] Abelson 20.

be responsive to the membership, their priorities were assessed at the first general assembly of the UJC.

According to J.J. Goldberg of *The Jerusalem Post*, the delegates attending each session at the first general assembly of the United Jewish Communities in 1999 told us what we need to know about the future direction of Jewish philanthropy.[28] According to those figures, the priorities should be Jewish renaissance and identity, fund-raising, Israel and overseas needs and social services, in that order.[29] The UJC has launched several new initiatives since then: a UJC-sponsored website with television listings and enticing interviews; identification of and contact with unaffiliated high-tech entrepreneurs; an attempt to link donors with similar interests and programs to educate young donors about Jewish causes.[30]

In an article published in 2001, UJC President and Chief Executive Officer Stephen Solender acknowledges the organization's growing pains and identifies two seemingly contradictory roles and goals of the new organization; to lead and to serve.[31] He agrees with Goldberg's assertion that the most important role for the UJC is to connect more Jewish people to the Jewish community and he cites examples of how the organization is serving as a catalyst to do just that.[32] Solender claims that in the nearly two years since its inception, the UJC has surpassed fund-raising expectations, led the North American Jewish response to the dissolving peace process in the Middle East, led the financial support to bring Ethiopian Jews to Israel and provided funding to relief efforts across Eastern Europe and the former Soviet Union.[33]

At home, UJC has partnered to make possible the Birthright Israel program, is in the process of conducting a Jewish population survey and is working in Washington, D.C., to enact laws and protect public policies on behalf of the Jewish community.[34]

---

[28] Goldberg 6.
[29] Goldberg 6.
[30] Miller B1.
[31] Stephen D. Solender, "Working on Our Identity, and Yours," *Forward* 6 Apr. 2001: 1-12.
[32] Solender 1-12.
[33] Solender 1-12.
[34] Solender 1-12.

If Solender is correct, the UJC is off and running and the record of its progress will speak for itself.

However, the UJC in creating an organization that improves on its predecessor must also be responsive to one of its largest constituencies: women.

New Players

In almost any discussion of modern Jewish life, one hears about the changing role of women, the need to attract the interest of our young people and the shifting focus of our community priorities. Philanthropy is no exception. American Jewish women have historically participated in fund-raising, advocacy and other philanthropic pursuits, but their role has traditionally been that of the unpaid volunteer.[35]   In our chapter on Politics, we have discussed how the contribution of women and women's organizations have, traditionally, gone unrecognized. Moreover, women have frequently had no or only token involvement in the organizations' power structures, even when women founded the organizations or when the goals were aimed toward the needs of women.[36]

This gender inequality recently began to change; consequently, women are now definitely among some of the newest faces in the world of philanthropy, most notably in positions of leadership. Martha Selig recalls an opening at the UJA-Federation of New York during the 1970s where "they told me that they couldn't offer me the executive position because I was a woman. One of the men asked, 'Well, how would it look if you walked out of the president's home late, at 11 o'clock at night after a meeting?' "[37]

In the year 2000, however, Janet Engelhart was named vice president of the Jewish Federation of Rhode Island, becoming the only female professional at the helm of a large Federation.[38] Her appointment demonstrates the beginnings of a changing role.

---

[35] Susan M. Chambré, "Parallel Power Structures, Invisible Careers and the Changing Nature of American Jewish Women's Philanthropy," *Journal of Jewish Communal Service* 76.3 (2000): 205-206.

[36] Chambré 205-206.

[37] Ami Eden, "Overturning Federation 'Boys Clubs' Is Big Charity's Surprise New Agenda," *Forward* 6 Oct. 2000: 1-12.

[38] Julie Wiener, "Beyond the Glass Ceiling," *Jewish Journal of Greater Los Angeles* 6 Oct. 2000.

Among the flood of phone calls she received following the announcement were those from other female professionals at Jewish organizations asking her to be their mentor.[39] Hopefully the promise of opening doors and other female role models will encourage some of these mid-level professionals to stay in the field, rather than abandon Jewish communal service in the hope of advancement. There is still a tremendous distance to be made up.

Whereas women, according to consultant Shifra Bronznick, hold 51 percent of all CEO posts at foundations, women run only two of the 40 major national Jewish organizations. Karen Winnick of the Winnick Family Foundation and Rachel Levin of the Righteous Persons Foundation in Los Angeles are two women serving their community from this type of local leadership position. Moreover, "virtually every profession and industry has moved more quickly and more effectively on opening opportunities to women at top levels," according to Louise Stoll, chief operating officer of the United Jewish Communities and herself the first woman to hold so high a position in the Federation world.[40] Nonetheless, gender equity may be on the way. One organizational leader argues that the community is now poised to close the gap and notes that half of the funded agencies have a female in the second spot.[41]

Women are also beginning to affect policy-making behind the scenes. The first initiative of the Trust for Jewish Philanthropy is a multistage plan called Advancing Women Professionals and the Jewish Community.[42] The project aimed at helping the Jewish community "identify, recruit, advance and retain women in management and executive positions" is partially funded by a grant from Barbara Dobkin and her husband, Eric, philanthropists known for their support of feminist causes.[43] Shifra Bronznick, a consultant, and Cindy

---

[39] Wiener, *Jewish Journal of Greater Los Angeles* 6 Oct. 2000.
[40] Julie Wiener, "Jewish Philanthropy: The Next Generation," *Jewish Funders Network Quarterly Newsletter*, Spring (2000).
[41] Eden 1-12.
[42] Eden 1-12.
[43] Wiener, *Jewish Funders Network Quarterly Newsletter, Spring* (2000).

Chazan, a Wexner Foundation official, have both been credited with contributing to the design of the initiative and are working with community leaders to establish guidelines that will attract female candidates.[44]

Jeffrey Solomon, president of the Andrea and Charles Bronfman Philanthropies who also helped design the project, recognizes the difficulties involved in gaining the establishment's cooperation. "When you operate an all-boys club," says Solomon, "you don't even notice that no women are at the table." Solomon believes the involvement of the trust may help to mainstream the issue, bringing it to the attention of the Jewish community.[45]

Success of the initiative to attract and empower women will depend on several factors, including financial and ideological support. Additional hurdles will involve recruiting and advancing female executives and modifying old patterns to make positions in Jewish communal service more attractive to qualified women. Audrey Weiner, executive vice president of New York's Jewish Home and Hospital for the Aging, questions "why many organizations can't seem to identify successful women from within the field."[46] Many believe the prior failures to promote have scared away potential candidates. Others, such as Sheila Bahat of the American Jewish Committee, suggest that women who have been considered for top positions sometimes decline to leave more time for family.[47] In response, Cindy Chazan hopes the new initiative will better the working conditions for everyone, bringing the community to conclude, "We have to respect and treat our executives in a whole new way in order to attract quality men and women, and to keep them."[48]

Women are also affecting Jewish philanthropy from without, harnessing the power of their pocketbooks. Not only are organizations realizing they need to target their appeals to women, but that they must do so in ways entirely different from their

---

[44] Eden 1-12.
[45] Eden 1-12.
[46] Eden 1-12.
[47] Wiener, *Jewish Funders Network Quarterly Newsletter, Spring* (2000).
[48] Eden 1-12.

appeals to men. Eve Landau, executive director of Ma'yan: The Jewish Women's Project, has found "there is more awareness in Jewish life about tapping into women's experience, but it's not yet happening in terms of funding."[49] She and Ma'yan founder Barbara Dobkin have been disappointed by the lack of financial support from the women who attend their popular feminist seders and have, along with researchers, concluded "that a lot of progressive women don't give Jewishly, while traditional Jews don't give progressively."[50]

Susan Weidman Schneider, editor-in-chief of *Lillith* magazine, found through extensive interviews that women today control more wealth than ever before, but their giving moves in the opposite direction from men's. Women, she discovered, tend to volunteer time first and money later, determining the amounts based on personal connectedness with the recipients more than the social status of the person asking. In addition, she determined that whereas men give to preserve institutions, Jewish women are interested in funding ideas and the creation of new programs.[51] Finally, women are looking beneath the surface to support the projects, programs, institutions and organizations that share their values, but also ones whose personal policies have a positive effect on women.

In the Jewish Funders Network newsletter, Zelda Stern advises women to examine their giving through a "gender lens," viewing issues that belong to the entire Jewish community with an eye toward their impact on girls and women.[52] She stresses asking questions to determine whether there are women in management positions, opportunities for flex-time, salaries commensurate with men and programs that serve women. Stern also emphasizes the power of collective giving and collective activism, forming partnerships for change and, when the answers aren't satisfactory, taking the money elsewhere.[53]

[49] Lawrence Bush and Jeffrey Dekro, "Funding Jewish Feminism," *Tikkun* 14.1 (1999): 44.
[50] Bush and Dekro 44.
[51] Bush and Dekro 44.
[52] Zelda Stern, "On Making Change: The Power of the Purse," *Jewish Funders Network Quarterly Newsletter*, Spring (2000).
[53] Stern, *Jewish Funders Network Quarterly Newsletter*, Spring (2000).

Despite the UJC's attempts to be more responsive and address the criticisms of the old Federation system and to find ways to cultivate new donors and allow them to better target the impact of their donations, many American Jews are still choosing to be philanthropic outside the UJC network in new and innovative ways. Consider Randall Kaplan, in his early 30s, entrepreneur, venture capitalist and founder of the Justice Ball fund-raiser benefiting the Bet Tzedek legal aid program of the Jewish Federation of Greater Los Angeles.

The Justice Ball is a successful charity event where the majority of attendees are under 40, and a significant portion are in their late 20s. Kaplan, a determined and charismatic young professional, is instrumental to the effort beyond his financial backing and organizational skills. Raphael Fogel, senior vice president and portfolio manager at SunAmerica, states, "What Randy does well is that ... he brings people together who can carry out that vision." [54]

Randall Kaplan is not from a wealthy family, but he learned his philanthropy at his mother's knee, so to speak. Kaplan states his mother was involved in charity work during his childhood and she describes his lifelong compassion for those less fortunate. [55] Another of Kaplan's mentors, Eli Broad, is a well-known philanthropic leader in Los Angeles whom Kaplan strives to emulate. Typical of his generation, however, Kaplan does not choose to give through a foundation but, instead, chooses direct involvement in what he calls "a real organization that helps real people." Most outstanding about Kaplan's success, where those before him failed, is that his vision has managed to involve a younger generation of donors, getting their commitment, their interest and single-handedly raising Bet Tzedek's profile as well as the bottom line. [56]

Innovative young American Jews are beginning to shape the future of Jewish giving. In another example, Los Angeles Dodger Shawn Green claims if he had a dollar for every bar mitzvah he

---

[54] Michael Aushenker, "Having a Ball," *Jewish Journal of Greater Los Angeles* 21 Jul. 2000.

[55] Aushenker, *Jewish Journal of Greater Los Angeles* 21 Jul. 2000.

[56] Aushenker, *Jewish Journal of Greater Los Angeles* 21 Jul. 2000.

was invited to during his first five years in the major leagues, he'd be rich – and he is.[57] Aside from the enticing contract, part of Green's decision to return to Los Angeles was a desire to sign with a team in a city that has a major Jewish population. This is part of Green's ongoing discovery of what it means to be a Jew, one of the identity issues gaining extra attention in recent years.[58] While aware of his Jewishness growing up, it was not until Green realized his position as a role model that he began to think about where he could make an impact. Green has already committed $1.5 million to the Dodgers' Dream Foundation and states a particular interest in setting up a charitable foundation to give even more to Jewish philanthropies.[59]

What Randall Kaplan and others have demonstrated is that there is a viable donor base among the young and newly rich. However, gaining their involvement requires creativity. One approach, as at the USC Casden Institute, is to invite interested young people to serve on a board and seek their suggestions for appropriate programming. Ray Kurtzman, chair of the Casden Institute Advisory Board, recruited siblings Chip and Cara Robertson during the 2000-01 academic year. The Robertsons' participation has opened the door for 20-somethings' participation in the institute from coast to coast.

Community building is also a priority, according to Seth Moskowitz of the American Associates of Ben-Gurion University of the Negev. For the American students who attend the institute, involvement begins in the classroom. When they return to the United States, they are walking emissaries for the university and for Israel, key participants in raising the $25 million in annual donations.[60]

For 30-something British financial investor Nigel Savage, the obstacles to getting projects underway in the Jewish community came as a surprise. In response, he created Hazon, an organization to help cultivate and fund new Jewish projects that may have

[57] Michael Bamberger and David Sabino, "Promised Land," *Sports Illustrated* 13 Dec 1999: 52-55.
[58] Bamberger and Sabino 52-55.
[59] Bamberger and Sabino 52-55.
[60] Bamberger and Sabino 52-55.

difficulty obtaining traditional funding. Savage and a handful of others are applying the know-how gained from the business world to empower young people and tap into the activities and issues of interest to them, such as a bike ride to promote awareness of Judaism and the environment.[61]

The need to attract more women and younger donors is not lost on the Federation. In New York, the UJA has created "@Home with YLD," a program of the Young Leadership Division of UJA-Federation of New York that has attracted younger members by sponsoring cocktail parties featuring promotional videos of their trips to Israel.[62]

In the style dubbed "venture philanthropy," donors are now "partners," grants are "investments" and the goal of "social return" is stressed through training and mentorship as much as through dollars. Will semantics bring support? Time will tell. However, the old organizations are making the effort. In the words of Martin Kaminer, 33-year-old JFN board member who is working with the Jewish Education Service of North America and the United Jewish Communities to create an incubator project, "No committees were involved. This is not the result of a study calling for new organizations.... We're learning as we go along."[63]

The Money

Philanthropy at its basest level is about raising money. We would be remiss if our review neglected the tremendous impact one particular member of the Jewish faith had on fund-raising for the Democratic Party. Probably no single event had so large an effect as the nomination of Senator Joseph Lieberman for the Democratic vice presidency during the year 2000 election campaign. Senator Lieberman, whose candidacy we examine in our Politics chapter, was the cause of a surge in contributions to the Democratic Party during the election year. Whether donors drew their inspiration from his character, his heritage or his politics, they all drew out their checkbooks and started to write.

[61] Wiener, *Jewish Funders Network Quarterly Newsletter,* Spring (2000).
[62] Aliza Phillips, "'Awesome' Soft Sell Lures Young Givers," *Forward* 10 Nov. 2000.
[63] Phillips, 10 Nov. 2000.

Marvin Lender of the bagel fortune had never directed his energy toward politics before. Yet, when he learned of Lieberman's selection, he began to fund-raise.[64] Even before calling on his large network of personal contacts, Lender was not alone.

Jewish Americans have long been supportive of the Democratic Party, but their contributions in the fall of 2000 provided "an unexpected infusion of hard money into the campaign," according to Melvin Levine, attorney and former congressman who campaigns for the Democratic National Committee (DNC) in Southern California.[65] Much of the fanfare is word of mouth, as the DNC does not actually track donations by religious or ethnic group, but DNC spokeswoman Jennifer Backus did confirm having received numerous telephone inquiries from Jews claiming a newfound interest in political donations.[66] Somewhat more surprising were the other politicians who traded political loyalties for religious ones. Rosalie Zalis, a registered Republican and former aide to California Governor Pete Wilson, told the *L.A. Times*, "This is a historic time for Jewish people. For me to say that [Lieberman's Jewishness] had nothing to do with my thinking would be a bald-faced lie." [67] In the post-election aftermath, has the "Lieberman Effect" begun to wane? Not likely, based on the reaction we received when the senator visited Los Angeles in April 2001 to deliver the Third Annual Carmen and Louis Warschaw Distinguished Lecture for the Casden Institute. Fully booked within hours, the senator's address to nearly 500 people at USC was attended by several local philanthropists and the larger Jewish community, as well as students, faculty and the local and national press.

On a purely financial level, the first year post-merger proved successful for the renamed and reorganized United Jewish Communities (UJC). Ranked seventh in the *Chronicle of*

---

[64] Elizabeth Shogren, "Campaign 2000: Lieberman Lures a Wave of New Political Money," *Los Angeles Times* 28 Sep. 2000: A15.

[65] Shogren A15.

[66] Shogren A15.

[67] Shogren A15.

Philanthropy's annual listing of the 400 not-for-profit
organizations with the largest revenues from individual contribu-
tors, the UJC raised $524.3 million in 1999 even as the overall
number of Jewish organizations to make the top 400 was
dropping.[68] Observers of the overall trends in giving were not
surprised, and attributed the overall drop to assimilated
American Jews making larger contributions to secular causes.
David Mersky, a senior lecturer at Brandeis University, also notes
that endowments and campaigns that allow designated funding
are tending to do better in the current climate of giving.[69]

In a spring 2001 edition, an article in *The Jewish Journal of
Greater Los Angeles* interviewed local philanthropy leaders to
get their sense of the fund-raising outlook in the wake of a
slowing economy. Across the board, the view was optimistic.
Most acknowledged that it is too early to tell what the long-term
effect will be but reported being either on or ahead of schedule
so far this year.[70] Especially promising, according to Evan
Mendelson of the Jewish Funders Network, is the growth in
private foundations that give to Jewish causes. There has been a
greater than 60 percent increase since 1998 and those figures
don't even include supporting categories.[71] The supporting
categories, to which Mendelson refers, are the new funding
streams for federated giving. They include permanent
endowment funds, both restricted and unrestricted, participatory
funds such as donor-advised or philanthropic funds and
supporting foundations. As Donald Kent and Jack Wertheimer
conclude, the decentralization of Federation funds has prompted
major shifts in the way Federations see their roles. They are
increasingly becoming the facilitators for big givers rather than
the controllers of communal spending and this may in fact prove
healthy to the system, challenging the agencies to clarify their
mission and goals in order to win funding.[72]

[68] Julie Wiener, "UJC is 7th Largest U.S. Charity; Other Jewish Groups Fall Behind," *Jewish Journal of Greater Los Angeles* 10 Nov. 2000.
[69] Wiener, *Jewish Journal of Greater Los Angeles* 10 Nov. 2000.
[70] Melissa Minkin, "Jewish Giving Is Still Looking Good," *Jewish Journal of Greater Los Angeles* 4 May 2001: 10-11.
[71] Minkin 10-11.
[72] Donald Kent and Jack Wertheimer, "The Implications of New Funding Streams for the Federation System," *Journal of Jewish Communal Service* 76.1 (2000): 69-77.

Conflict of Interest

If Jewish participation in charity is a moral imperative, when is fund-raising immoral? This issue was neatly drawn when the UJA chose to honor Thomas Middelhoff, the chief executive of Bertelsmann, a German media conglomerate that during World War II published Nazi propaganda for Hitler's army.[73] Many of the issues raised by the choice of Middelhoff as honoree were the same as when Israel decided to accept reparations from Germany in 1965: Is the American Jewish community ready for some closure on the past and ready to move toward a new relationship with German companies? Also up for discussion is whether a corporate executive born after the fact should be held responsible for his company's past. Those who selected Mr. Middlehoff stressed that he ordered the investigation into Bertelsmann's past and has attempted to make reparations wherever possible.[74] However, this did not tame the outrage felt by many American Jews, some survivors or children of survivors, who saw the decision as placing financial concerns ahead of moral ones.

There were ardent arguments on both sides. "Should we wake up every morning and reindict?" asked Kenneth J. Bialkin, a New York lawyer who is active in Jewish causes. He continued, "I don't think we can afford the luxury of hating, of self-pity about the past." Gwendolyn Jacobs, an 83-year-old resident, says, "During the war we did not do enough, fast enough, to react to the horrors. We didn't do enough then, and if we accept this kind of thing, again we're not doing enough." In the end, the dinner was held and Elie Wiesel, a writer and Holocaust survivor, was the keynote speaker. Wiesel said he agreed to speak because he trusted Mr. Middlehoff. "While it was in the end Random House that gave the money for the survivors' memoirs, the agreement was with Bertelsmann, and it was Middlehoff who made the commitment," Wiesel said.[75]

---

[73] Tamar Lewin, "History Collides With Contrition as Jewish Group Honors a German," *New York Times* 30 Apr. 2001, late ed: B1.

[74] Lewin B1.

[75] Lewin B1.

The Mission

Defining the mission of Jewish philanthropy, particularly in
the absence of an obvious worldwide Jewish crisis, poses an
ongoing challenge to the Jewish community. By necessity, any
such mission must be broad enough to include all sectors of
American Jewry and yet precise enough to inform collective
actions. As with any mission, or belief system for that matter,
it is important that the statement portray the strength of its
convictions, yet its framing should allow the flexibility to adapt
during periods of change. This is all more daunting a task
because Jewish philanthropy must look to its future, not its past.
Philanthropic institutions cannot rely on what worked in the past,
but must ask: "What will work for the future?" Fortunately, a
number of funders and organizations have already begun to
focus on these issues, in some cases going as far as to create new
committees, organizations, and in one case, a new approach to
philanthropy to achieve these goals.

One aspect of the mission of Jewish philanthropy, according
to Gary A. Tobin, ought to be a move away from fear-based
donor motivation toward a more positive message. He asserts
that the crisis mentality remains at the core of fund-raising
efforts, with the leadership moving from a reliance on external
sources of danger as motivating factors to a focus on the internal
threat of Jewish assimilation.[76] Tobin identifies the weakness of
this approach, writing that the very crisis of continuity this
appeal would hope to address runs the risk of insufficient
funding due to the unappealing nature of the appeal itself. In
other words, if Jewish communal organizations hope to gain the
interest and contributions of America's more integrated, less
affiliated Jews, then the community organizations must create
vehicles for participation and giving that strengthen the bonds of
Jewish identity, rather than criticize and sensationalize the
threatening nature of their target group's lifestyle.[77] Lest he
himself only criticize, Tobin suggests a number of positive foci

---

[76] Gary A. Tobin, "In Integrated Age, Givers Want Meaning, Not Crisis," *Forward* 10 Nov. 2000.
[77] Tobin, *Forward* 10 Nov. 2000.

Jewish communal organizations might consider in order to compete with the pleas of more secular causes; all in the very American tradition of accentuating the positive. To name just a few, Tobin suggests supporting associations with Israel as a culturally enriching experience for world Jewry instead of as a mission of survival; promoting human services as a means of doing *tzedakah* — building one's covenantal relationship with God; and, finally, by embracing Jewish education as a means of personal and communal enlightenment, not as a prevention against assimilation.[78]

Tobin is certainly not alone in his call for more positive thinking. Ephraim Buchwald echoes his sentiments, in a talk on conversion and the American Jewish agenda (where, incidentally, he completely disagrees with Tobin on the topic of conversion). Buchwald states his outrage that "we're spending billions of dollars on Holocaust memorials, rather than investing our resources in joyous, Jewish outreach for our young people.... We and our children know only too well what it's like to be holed up in an attic in Amsterdam, to be shot in the head or buried alive at Babi Yar, and to be tortured at Ravensbruck. But do our young people know what it means to fervently sing L'cha Dodi, to welcome the Sabbath Bride ... to be embraced by a Jewish parent on Friday night ... to be in such high spirits on Purim that they don't know the difference between Mordechai and Haman?"[79] Buchwald claims there are millions of American Jews who want to be a part of the Jewish community, who may be only inches away, and it has been the failure to expose them to the joyous, optimistic side of Judaism that has led to the steady statistical decline of the Jewish community since the end of World War II.[80] Buchwald, like Tobin, also proposes the Jewish education solution, arguing that the strongest form of celebration is the teaching, inspiring and nurturing of the next generation of Jewish leaders and, yes, Jewish philanthropists.[81]

---

[78] Tobin, *Forward* 10 Nov. 2000.
[79] Ephraim Buchwald, "Conversion and the American Jewish Agenda," *Judaism* 48.3 (1999): 274-277.
[80] Buchwald 274-277.
[81] Buchwald 274-277.

As was made abundantly clear during the 2000 presidential campaigns, education continues to be an issue that concerns all Americans. Accordingly, Jewish education is receiving increasing philanthropic attention. Although we discuss these issues in greater detail in the Education chapter, many parents are showing the desire for their children and grandchildren to have a prominent Jewish education, oftentimes more than they themselves were provided. Generalized concern about assimilation and intermarriage has also contributed to the community interest, and several new schools have been built around the country in the past decade to meet this growing need. At the heart of this movement are some of the leading Jewish philanthropists: Michael Steinhardt, Edgar Bronfman and Charles Schusterman – three of the 12 founders of the Partnership for Excellence in Jewish Education (PEJE).

At last year's donor assembly sponsored by the PEJE, Los Angelenos such as Shirley and Aaron Kotler, Janine and Peter Lowy, Anton Gordon and Peter Rubin met with their counterparts from around the country to network and set the agenda for the "day school movement." [82] Out of these discussions came two priority items: raising additional funds and creating more awareness of the existence of and curriculum provided by Jewish day schools. In his keynote address, Jack Wertheimer urged the day school leaders to make a greater effort to sell their cause to Jewish family foundations, which at the time were giving less than half their money to Jewish causes and roughly 2 percent to day schools.[83] Day schools are not the only form of Jewish education, and the growing number of participants working toward better Hebrew school or after-school programs also demonstrates the relevance of a mission that includes enhancing the educational experience. Programs at colleges and universities, such as the Hillel movement, campus centers for Jewish student life and a number of more specialized Jewish research groups abound and individual projects such as

---

[82] Julie Wiener, "Spreading the Word: Donors Gather to Discuss the Jewish Day School Alternative," *Jewish Journal of Greater Los Angeles* 22 Sept. 2000.
[83] Wiener, *Jewish Journal of Greater Los Angeles* 22 Sept. 2000.

Avodah's service corps, bringing Jews together to learn community building techniques through the use of Jewish texts, continue to flourish. The prevailing notion seems to be that the more Jewish values are taught and inculcated, the more our community will benefit.

Certain funders seek to use Jewish philanthropy not only to express their Jewish values but also to create broader programs for social change. Although some would argue that turning away from specifically Jewish causes weakens our sense of community, the bulk of the evidence indicates otherwise. Rabbi David Rosenn of Avodah teaches that Jewish life sets its goal as taking part in something larger than our present imperfect reality, that very basic principles of Judaism embody the ideals of universal social justice and economic equality and that these basic principles do and should have broad implications for how American Jews spend their time, live their lives and allocate their disposable income.[84] This is not a new concept in Jewish thinking. Jews have historically been involved as social policy activists, communal workers, public officials and voters. Rabbi Abraham Joshua Heschel stressed the Jewish value in the fight for civil rights. The Reform movement has always emphasized the prophetic nature of protest and social change. What is new is the rapidly growing number of family foundations, donor-advised funds and other philanthropic structures choosing to explicitly address social issues from a Jewish standpoint as an expression of Jewish identity. Also new is the belief that working toward these broad-based societal goals is of equal importance to support for Israel, synagogue affiliation and promoting Jewish culture. Particularly new is the fact that support for these programs is outpacing the traditional communal allocations process of the Federation system as more and more American Jews choose to fund secular social causes in the name of Jewish values, goals and ideals.[85] So should the Jewish philanthropic mission include causes that are not necessarily Jewish? According to Evan Mendelson, "to play a constructive role in

---

[84] Groner 1-4.
[85] Groner 1-4.

Jewish community relations, the Federations should welcome the involvement of Jews in the society and global community in which they live." According to his belief, the philanthropic community will be more successful, more appreciated and more of a resource when it begins to encourage an integration of donors' Jewish, American and philanthropic selves.[86]

How can one community frame a dynamic mission that will incorporate uplifting messages and religious-based educational programs, as well as facilitate a synthesis of local and global, survival and renewal, Jewish and American, public and private issues? According to some of the leading philanthropists today, it is done by being very provocative and challenging and by raising the Jewish identity of Jews everywhere.[87] Michael Massing's article "Should Jews Be Parochial?" largely tells the story of modern Jewish philanthropy. That is, Michael Steinhardt's story. Steinhardt exemplifies the latest trends in Jewish philanthropy and, if he has any say in it, the way of the future. Since his retirement in 1995, Steinhardt has poured tens of millions of dollars into Jewish causes – all kinds of Jewish causes. Along with his colleagues, he makes no pretense about his desires, namely to kindle a Jewish renaissance and ultimately transform Jewish philanthropy.[88] Steinhardt isn't subtle and his approach incorporates much of what has already been suggested. In fact, a hallmark of his approach is how expansive and pervasive it's become. Steinhardt started the Jewish Life Network to promote Jewish identity and awareness; created a cultural center for Jewish singles; helped launch a program to send young Jews to Israel; helped form a campaign to revitalize America's synagogues; funded a network of Jewish outreach workers on college campuses; and formed a partnership to build Jewish day schools across the country.[89] The efforts of Steinhardt and a handful of others are not haphazard. They meet a few times

---

[86] Evan Mendelson, "The Funder's Perspective," *Journal of Jewish Communal Service* 76.1 (1999): 77-79.

[87] Karen W. Arenson, "Art, Wildlife and a Bit of Investing," *New York Times* 12 Nov. 2000, east coast late ed.: C2.

[88] Michael Massing, "Should Jews Be Parochial?," *The American Prospect* 11.23 (2000): 30-35.

[89] Massing 30-35.

a year to study, exchange ideas, evaluate progress, plan collaborations, discuss faith and discuss money. They are extremely influential en masse. They are thinking and talking about the future of American Jewry. Pioneering new techniques, orchestrating trends and helping to define the mission through their actions and their strategies, as well as their contributions, perhaps Steinhardt et al., really will create the uplifting, education-focused, broad-based mission statement that will lead to a Jewish renaissance.[90]

Challenges

Debates and policy changes in the larger community can also relate to challenges in the realm of Jewish philanthropy and vice versa. The benefactors and recipients of Jewish philanthropy, therefore, may explore from time to time the role of the organized community in matters beyond those that are explicitly Jewish in nature. For example, how do Jewish values and Jewish philanthropy fit in with the ongoing welfare policy debates in the U.S., Israel and other countries? How do the actions and reactions of the Jewish philanthropic community influence these debates and what message do these actions and reactions convey about the community's stance on this issue?

The welfare questions essentially bring us back to where we began the chapter, with the concepts of *tzedakah* and *tikkun olam*. One question in this debate is whether welfare policies should be universal or means-tested. That is, should a particular group receive benefits, possibly excluding needy non-members, or should only the truly needy receive benefits, allowing for preservation of precious resources? According to Rabbi Yedidya Sinclair, proponents of universal benefits believe that system is more dignified, less exclusionary and a right of citizenship. Conversely, supporters of means-testing argue for a system that they claim is more efficient as well as more stringent and one that helps contain costs in times of greater longevity and

[90] Massing 30-35.

long-term unemployment.[91] If one looks to Jewish sources, the obligation to give charity is of central importance, both through the commandment to give *tzedakah* and the realization that in supporting the needy we work toward *tikkun olam*. However, the emphasis on the shame and stigma attached to accepting charity, the injunction to the community against giving charity to people not in real need, and the explicit instruction to check a claimant's neediness in all cases except where the person is claiming food, demonstrate a Jewish dictum for the means-tested model.[92] Another, more general question about welfare policy is whether welfare benefits should be provided at all. Or is the welfare-state model, in its current iteration, the very antithesis of the Jewish charitable tradition? David Dalin argues that modern Jewish liberals have misunderstood the concept of *tzedakah*, overlooking the essential components of individual self-help and communal self-sufficiency. He proposes that, rather than extol increased government spending and social welfare programs, American Jews should recognize the religious preference for charitable lending and suggest this as a model that other communities might emulate.[93] Marshall Breger, a professor of law who was an aide to former President Reagan, concurs. He states, "In Jewish tradition, the poor and needy have a claim, as does every individual person, to *tzedakah*. But they don't have a preference. *Tzedakah* doesn't mean that you have to vote for welfare." Breger continues, "The right way to combat social inequalities may not be the liberation clichés of the left, but the personal responsibility that will get the poor out of poverty."[94]

As we near the end of this review, it should be obvious that the world of Jewish philanthropy is no longer an insular one. Issues that are prevalent in the larger society, such as conflicting business models, the role of women, the economy and new technology, are just as prevalent and true in the Jewish

[91] Rabbi Yedidya Sinclair, "Welfare: Universal or Means-Tested Benefits?," *Center for Business Ethics & Social Responsibility*.
[92] Sinclair, *Center for Business Ethics & Social Responsibility*.
[93] Dalin 28-33.
[94] Groner 1-4.

communal world. And issues that arise in Jewish communal policy also can have implications for the greater society and our secular lives.

American Jews continue to express a deep and sincere commitment to charity and philanthropy. Inspired by Jewish concepts of *tzedakah* and *tikkun olam*, there is a long tradition of giving which exists to this day. Jewish charitable organizations such as the Federations created at the beginning of the century to provide social services for emigrants and the UJA, created to rescue Jews from World War II, have merged to form the UJC. Their daunting task is to correct the mistakes of the past and make choices for the future. Criticized in the past for being unresponsive and uncreative, the UJC faces a new landscape of donors and philanthropy. Individual donors want more control over where their funds go, and there are a number of donors such as Alan Casden, Charles Bronfman and Michael Steinhardt who have helped created new institutes and charities to galvanize the Jewish community. Women need to be empowered and better recruited into the highest ranks of philanthropic organizations. At the same time, there is a new generation of young donors who are eager to create events and programming for their peers and can be effective in fund-raising, as evidenced by Randall Kaplan's Justice Ball for Bet Tzedek. Finally, although the UJC continues to be successful on a purely financial level, having been ranked seventh in the *Chronicle of Philanthropy's* annual listing of the top 400 not-for-profits by contribution, Jewish philanthropy must look to the future, emphasizing positive messages, focusing on Jewish education and following the example set by such philanthropists as Michael Steinhardt, creating new initiatives for funders to express themselves Jewishly while creating programs for social change.

Chapter Four

EDUCATION:
Jewish Continuity in the 21ˢᵗ Century

Overall, American Jewish education has never been healthier; however, a sense of crisis exists. In 1990, a survey found that the rate of assimilation and intermarriage had increased substantially. For many, the solution to Jewish continuity lies in Jewish education and Jewish day schools; therefore, while education continues to be one of the major concerns for most Americans, Jews in particular have a vested interest in this issue.

During the 2000 presidential campaign, education was among the candidates' top priorities, and the issues of school choice and school vouchers were highly debated. We will survey the arguments of various scholars for and against school vouchers, particularly in the context of Jewish education. Beyond the intellectual arguments, there are many commentators who believe that American Jews in particular should support school vouchers to bolster Jewish day schools. Jewish day schools have increased in popularity and many argue that they are one of the most effective ways to promote Jewish values. We will examine the theories scholars and commentators have given for this growth. Yet, for reasons we will explore in this chapter, American Jews remain committed to public education and supplementary Jewish education. We will review the history and patterns of American Jewish education to understand this issue better and to review innovative suggestions to ensure continuity and improve Jewish education in the 21st Century.

American Jews & Education

As Susan Laemmle, USC's Dean of Religious Life, noted in a recent article, "In the last half century, we Jews have been increasingly present and increasingly prominent on American campuses. . . . In recent years Jews have assumed the presidencies of important, prestigious citadels of higher education, including those – like Princeton, which were once entered only within strict quotas."[1] Universities and colleges such as Harvard, Dartmouth, Williams and Barnard have all had Jewish presidents in recent years. As Laemmle notes, "At USC, a Jewish executive vice provost is joined by a large contingent of Jewish deans and many Jewish faculty members."[2] Rabbi Laemmle is not alone in holding the title of Dean of Religious Life at a major university. In the 1980s, Rabbi Michael Paley became chaplain of Columbia, thus becoming the first Jew in charge of overall religious life at an American college or university.[3] Currently, Rabbi Patricia Karlin-Neumann holds the title of Associate Dean of Religious life at Stanford University.[4]

It is not just the presence of American Jews at the highest levels of academe that give a special topicality to this chapter. In

---

[1]   Susan Laemmle, "Campus Rabbi With a Difference: Notes From a Jewish Dean of Religious Life," *CCAR: A Reform Jewish Quarterly* (2000): 30.
[2]   Laemmle 30.
[3]   Laemmle 30.
[4]   Laemmle 30.

the last year, national concerns and Jewish concerns have found common cause in education issues. President George W. Bush has said, "Education is my top priority."[5] During the campaign, both candidate Bush and Vice President Gore were vocal about education and religion (we discuss the latter at greater length in the Politics chapter). During and since the campaign, the intersection of religion and education has centered on the issue of school vouchers.

School vouchers have been highly debated in the Jewish community. As we will outline below, there are many cogent arguments for and against school vouchers. The issue was debated in an evening at USC co-hosted by the Casden Institute, and we will share the insights of debaters Professor Erwin Chemerinsky of USC and Professor Eugene Volokh of UCLA. However, beyond the intellectual arguments, within the Jewish community there has been a strong movement to support school vouchers as a way of strengthening participation in Jewish day schools.

To understand the increase in day schools' popularity, we need to view it in the context of changes in Jewish attitudes about education over the last century, particularly over the last decade. The rise of Jewish day schools is a phenomenon of our times and is symptomatic of larger issues and fears at play in the world of Jewish education. To some, Jewish day schools are the only way to ensure Jewish continuity; however, the statistics on which many base this belief may not present the whole picture. Is it possible that day schools may be no more effective a salve for inter-marriage than other approaches? Closer scrutiny may lead us to conclude that it is more important to ensure Jewish peer group interaction in the teen years, as part of either formal or informal Jewish education to treat "at-risk youth." Regardless of how it is achieved, it is incumbent upon Jewish educators to acknowledge that the majority of Jewish children will experience some form of supplemental education and to fashion a vision for the 21st century.

---

[5] Molly Parker, "Bush Discusses Plan for American People," *Daily Egyptian* [Carbondale] 1 March 2001.

School Vouchers: Pros and Cons

Parents want a say in their children's education. Government wants to provide the best education possible. How to accomplish both of these goals is a matter of great debate. School vouchers and school choice have become hot button issues, addressed by all politicians. The debate about whether or not parents should be able to send children to the school of their choice, religious or not, and receive money from the government to do so not only generates strong emotions but also raises a legal debate. The eloquent support on both sides of the issue was evident at the September 2000 event hosted by the Casden Institute at USC, where both positions were elucidated.[6] Co-sponsored by the Hebrew Union College, the debate featured USC Law Professor Erwin Chemerinsky arguing against and UCLA Law Professor Eugene Volokh arguing in favor of school vouchers. Carmen Warschaw moderated the debate.

Professor Chemerinsky teaches administrative law, constitutional law, federal courts and procedures at USC; he specializes in constitutional law and civil rights issues. His recent published works include *Constitutional Law: Principles and Policies; Interpreting the Constitution; Federal Jurisdiction;* "The Values of Federalism" and "The First Amendment: When the Government Must Make Content Based Choices." Professor Chemerinsky argued that vouchers are unconstitutional.[7] He articulated that school vouchers represent a government subsidy of religious institutions, and as such they violate the First Amendment-mandated separation of church and state.[8] Vouchers also violate Supreme Court precedents that forbid transfer of government funds to religious institutions.[9] School vouchers are also troubling, Chemerinsky argued, because they afford no government oversight of spending in private institutions.[10] As a result, the voucher school's curricula could be

---

[6] Erwin Chemerinsky, address, "Conference on School Voucher Initiative: Should There Be a Jewish Position?", University of Southern California, Los Angeles, 11 Sept. 2000.

[7] Chemerinsky 11 Sept. 2000.

[8] Chemerinsky 11 Sept. 2000.

[9] Chemerinsky 11 Sept. 2000.

[10] Chemerinsky 11 Sept. 2000.

racist, homophobic or anti-Semitic. Chemerinsky next argued
that school voucher programs would be detrimental to the public
educational system in several ways. First of all, a lack of
oversight marginalizes small religious and ethnic groups by
funneling the large majority of funds into mainstream religious
and private institutions.[11] The financial consequences could have
negative social results. One possible result is that middle- and
upper-class students would take the majority of enrollment slots
at desirable institutions, leaving poorer students in schools that
cost less, and those poorer schools therefore also would provide
fewer academic resources to their students.[12] The lack of
enforceable standards in private education could lead to
profiteering by institutions that would seek to provide the bare
minimum education in an effort to retain a portion of the voucher
payment as profit. Furthermore, he argues that the school voucher
program is a poor public spending initiative due to its lack of
oversight. Finally, the voucher program lacks enforcement of
current laws; for example, there are no plans for education of
handicapped and disabled students.[13]

The arguments in favor of vouchers, as put forward by
Professor Volokh, are equally compelling.[14] Professor Volokh
teaches free speech law, copyright law, the law of government
and religion, and a seminar on firearms regulation policy at UCLA
Law School. Before coming to UCLA, he served as clerk for
U.S. Supreme Court Justice Sandra Day O'Connor and Judge
Alex Kozinski on the U.S. 9th Circuit Court of Appeals. He is
the author of a wide body of law review articles and opinion
editorials, including "Why School Choice Is Constitutional"
(originally published in *The New Republic*) and a longer piece on
the same subject called "Equal Treatment Is Not Establishment."

Professor Volokh stated that public schools are failing our
children.[15] There are several indicators to support this claim.

---

[11] Chemerinsky 11 Sept. 2000.
[12] Chemerinsky 11 Sept. 2000.
[13] Chemerinsky 11 Sept. 2000.
[14] Eugene Volokh, address, "Conference on School Voucher Initiative: Should There Be a Jewish Position?", University of Southern California, Los Angeles, 11 Sept. 2000.
[15] Volokh 11 Sept. 2000.

Professor Volokh argued that, although spending in the past two decades has doubled, there has been no discernable increase in the quality of education. This crisis in the quality of education demands alternatives for our children. There is every reason to believe that, as in other areas, choice driven by competition will ensure and promote quality in education. Volokh argued that vouchers make education more equitable by giving choice to all. Currently, given the high costs of private education, choice in education belongs to the affluent. Why shouldn't parents with lower incomes have some choice, rather than none at all? Although vouchers will not give the same choice to all, at least it gives all some choice.[16]

Volokh's next point was that money should follow students, not support a bureaucracy.[17] He disputed the contention that somehow school vouchers are akin to giving away "the bank" to the rich. Vouchers, Volokh argued, are significantly more valuable to the poor than to the rich.[18] He disputed the claim that school voucher programs would lead to the deterioration of the public school system. Fewer students in public school means that there is less of a financial and administrative burden on the school system, and public school students would benefit from a system that is less strained for resources.[19] Finally, Volokh suggested that we should keep focused on our priority: the children rather than the schools. Money needs to be spent on the children, not on upholding an archaic bureaucracy.[20]

As to the question of constitutionality, Professor Volokh had three major points. First of all, one can argue that the current state of education discriminates against institutions based on religious affiliation. Why should a school be denied funds because of its religious affiliation? This idea is inherently unconstitutional.[21] Second, primary education has been unfairly singled out. Presently, private and secular colleges receive federal funding, charitable donations to religiously affiliated

---

[16] Volokh 11 Sept. 2000.
[17] Volokh 11 Sept. 2000.
[18] Volokh 11 Sept. 2000.
[19] Volokh 11 Sept. 2000.
[20] Volokh 11 Sept. 2000.
[21] Volokh 11 Sept. 2000.

institutions are tax deductible, and even welfare recipients can give their federal grant money to churches as tithes. So why deny primary schools federal funds because of their parochial ties? [22] Finally, Professor Volokh argues that school vouchers maintain government neutrality by giving the choice to the individual and constitute no breach of the separation between church and state.[23]

School Vouchers:
How Should American Jews View the Issue?

The debate on school vouchers was held not only on college campuses but also in political and academic journals. Both Jack Wertheimer in *Commentary* and Jeremy Rabkin in *Policy Review* argued that American Jews should support school vouchers. Rabkin cites two main grounds of opposition among Jewish groups:

> On the one hand, there is skepticism that many more Jewish parents would send their children to separate Jewish schools, even if some form of public funding made them more affordable. On the other hand, there is concern that government aid to or "entanglement" with religious schools would foster a more religious atmosphere in the country, which would be, in practice, a Christian atmosphere, hence marginalizing to non-Christian groups. Many Jewish organizations are staunch advocates of public education, seeing it as a guarantor of a common public culture, which ensures toleration for religious minorities.[24]

Rabkin feels these concerns are misplaced in contemporary America.[25] Voucher subsidies, he believes, might convince many Jewish parents to send their children to day school.[26] As support, Rabkin cites the experience of the Samis Foundation in

---

[22] Volokh 11 Sept. 2000.
[23] Volokh 11 Sept. 2000.
[24] Jeremy Rabkin, "A Choice for the Chosen," *Policy Review* 108.5 (1999): 37-40.
[25] Rabkin 37-40.
[26] Rabkin 37-40.

Seattle. In a 1995 Seattle survey commissioned by the Samis
Foundation, one-third of the 419 families contacted who did not
send their children to Jewish day school said they were
considering doing so, and half of those said they would pay as
much as $3,000 for such a school. The Samis Foundation then
arranged with the only Jewish high school in Seattle to cap its
tuition at $3,000, providing assistance beyond that. The result,
Rabkin reports, was an immediate 34% jump in enrollment.[27]
Although that statistic only reflected an actual increase from 54
to 78 students, it was a significant indicator. As for concerns
about the dangers of creating a more "religious atmosphere,"
Rabkin sees this attitude as passé. "There is no reliable evidence
to substantiate the concern that Christian religious education will
foster intolerance." [28] Furthermore, since public schools now
promote multiculturalism, the notion of the common public
education is long gone anyway.

Jack Wertheimer views the Jewish community that has thus
far failed to support school vouchers for day schools as
"shortsighted and hypocritical." [29] Wertheimer, while agreeing
with both of Rabkin's arguments, also feels that day schools must
be supported in order to ensure the future of the Jewish
community.[30] Wertheimer maintains that there are threats to
Jewish continuity (assimilation and intermarriage) and the best
weapon against it is Jewish education fostered specifically in
Jewish day schools. "That the Jewish day school has 'proved
itself' seems beyond dispute," Wertheimer says.[31] Rather than
accepting Wetheimer's assertion at face value, let us draw our
own conclusions after considering Jewish education and Jewish
day schools within the context of the past few decades.

A Sense of Crisis in Jewish Education

The work of Wertheimer, Rabkin and authors published in
conservative journals may indicate that Jewish education was

---

[27] Rabkin 37-40.
[28] Rabkin 37-40.
[29] Jack Wertheimer, "Who's Afraid of Jewish Day Schools?" *Commentary* (New York: Dec 1999): 49-53.
[30] Wertheimer 49-53.
[31] Wertheimer 49-53.

bereft and broken, collapsing under the weight of its own failures. Despite this seemingly pervasive sense of crisis, however, it remains true that education is a deeply rooted and immutable facet of what it means to be Jewish. One cannot approach the subject of Jewish education, or the role of American Jews in education, without being impressed and overwhelmed. The attention, effort, study, conferences and publications are extensive, giving greater meaning to the appellation of Jews as "The People of the Book."

Much credit for the explosion in the serious study of Jewish education belongs to the Jewish Education Service of North America (JESNA). Although it feels like JESNA has always been part of the landscape of Jewish education, in fact the organization was only created in 1981.[32] JESNA is the Federations' educational coordinating, planning and development agency. They strive to improve the quality and affordability of Jewish day schools and work closely to recruit, develop, train and reward Jewish educators. Finally, they try to use research to foster continuous improvement.[33]

JESNA sponsors the Network for Research in Jewish Education ("the Network") and its sometimes-provocative newsletter. Carol K. Ingall, JESNA chair and an associate professor of Jewish education at the Jewish Theological Seminary (JTS), has a front-page column that is as challenging as it is enlightening. For example, a recent column discussed how the same principles a mathematics professor uses with her graduate students should be used for students in Jewish studies:

> Lampert defines the moral qualities embedded in the acquiring of mathematical knowledge: intellectual courage (readiness to revise our beliefs), intellectual honesty (changing our beliefs when there is a good reason to do so), and wise restraint (not changing a belief without some good reason and/or serious examination).[34]

---

[32] JESNA. Fall 2001, <http:// www.jesna.org>.
[33] JESNA. Fall 2001, <http:// www.jesna.org>.
[34] Carol K. Ingall, "The Ethics of Research," *Newsletter of the Network for Research in Jewish Education* [New York]: 16.

For the past 15 years, JESNA has also sponsored a yearly conference in which professors, graduate students, researchers and practitioners all participate. In addition to the diverse paper presentations, there are many panels and sessions on a full array of topics of Jewish learning. The June 2000 conference in New York was hosted by the JTS and attended by more than 100 participants, making for a resounding statement as to the vibrancy of Jewish education.[35] There was a session led by Bethamie Horowitz, whose recent book, *Connections and Journeys: Assessing Critical Opportunities of Enhancing Jewish Identity,* explored Jewish identity as it changes over a lifetime, and one by Barry Holtz, who led a study of midrashic text that facilitated a discussion of educational issues.[36] Seventeen papers were presented, ranging from a discussion of whether the attrition in Jewish supplementary school education occurs following the period of bar/bat mitzvah also means a disengagement from continued informal Jewish education, to a paper titled, "How Children Conceptualize God," in which nearly 1,000 third- through seventh-graders were studied.[37] Even more participants, papers and sessions were expected for the 2001 conference.

Despite all this activity, there continues to be a sense of crisis among observers of Jewish education. In 1995, Dr. Jonathan Woocher, the executive vice president of JESNA, sounded a note of alarm in an article titled, "Jewish Education: Crisis and Vision." [38] Woocher pointed to several weaknesses in Jewish education. First, he argues that the Jewish educational mission is vague because its goals are so confused.[39] Is the goal a successful bar/bat mitzvah? Someone who can pray in Hebrew? Someone who won't intermarry? Woocher concludes that we are in dire need of consensus.[40] Similarly, he argues that our standards of what constitutes an educated Jew are too low.

---

[35] Ingall 16.
[36] Ingall 16.
[37] Ingall 16.
[38] Jonathan Woocher, "Jewish Education: Crisis and Vision," *JESNA Publications* 13 (1995).
[39] Woocher, *JESNA Publications* 13 (1995).
[40] Woocher, *JESNA Publications* 13 (1995).

Since the educational goals are unclear, there is no agreement on what to teach. As a result, there is too often a "smorgasbord approach: a little Hebrew, a little Bible, a little history and a few religious concepts and skills." [41]   Finally, Woocher asks why anyone would want to be a Jewish educator: "They are not leaders in the community, not particularly well-paid, nor particularly involved in the greater community that surrounds them." [42] These criticisms apply equally to adult Jewish education. Without a clear image of Jewish adulthood, writes Sheldon Dorph, "the direction, purposes, and methods of Jewish education – schooling or otherwise – become unclear." [43]

Why is everyone so worried? Part of the reason appears to be the 1990 National Jewish Population Survey (NJPS) that revealed an increased rate of intermarriage and assimilation. Since then, two sets of researchers have used the NJPS statistics to attempt to identify what best to do about this situation. At the same time, for a number of reasons to be discussed below, the number of Jewish day schools has increased in the United States. As we approached the end of the 20th century, many sought to link intermarriage and day schools. Could the lack of one (day school education) be the cause of the other (increased intermarriage rates)? To understand why this seems conceivable, we must consider day schools in the context of Jewish and public education in America.

Patterns of American Jewish Education

There is no question that there has been a dramatic increase in day schools in America. In the 1940s, there were fewer than 20,000 students attending full-time Jewish day schools. Today, the number is closer to 200,000, and there are more than 700 schools nationwide. [44] In the first decades of this century, the notion of separate schools was an anathema to most Jewish leaders. The United States was a melting pot, and the goal was to

---

[41] Woocher, *JESNA Publications* 13 (1995).
[42] Woocher, *JESNA Publications* 13 (1995).
[43] Woocher, *JESNA Publications* 13 (1995).
[44] Wertheimer 49-53.

become accepted in the mainstream of American society. Jewish day schools were not perceived as part of that plan. In 1908, Samson Benderly, later the director of the Board of Education of the New York Kehillah, an early Jewish community organization, argued that for Jews to keep their Jewishness among the larger American society, "a parochial system of education among the Jews would be fatal to such hopes." [45] This opinion did not change much in the next 50 years. In 1956, the American Council for Judaism restated its opposition to schools that "take children out of the general American environment and train them to lead segregated lives." [46] Public education was seen as the great equalizer, an institution in which children of all faiths could participate. For many Jews, the public schools became a route to rapid Americanization and to academic and professional success. In the words of Alvin I. Schiff, Yeshiva University's Irving I. Stone Professor of Education, "[The public school system] was the method and setting by which Jews could become Americans." [47] Or, as one Jewish leader put it, "[the schools were a place where] the children of the high and low, rich and poor, Protestant, Catholics and Jews mingle together, play together and are taught that we are a free people, striving to elevate mankind and respect each other." [48]

For the religious education of their children, the great majority of American Jews chose "supplemental education," a Protestant notion that public schooling itself was non-denominational; religious education was left to after-school hours and weekends. As Peter Beinart articulated in *The Atlantic Monthly*, even as the public schools fostered upward mobility, the supplementary schools would instill in Jewish children "sufficient knowledge and group attachment to prevent integration from becoming assimilation." [49] At least that was the theory. However, in the second half of the 20th century a number

[45] Peter Beinart, "The Rise of Jewish Schools," *The Atlantic Monthly* 284.4 (1999): 21-22.
[46] Beinart 21-22.
[47] Beinart 21-22.
[48] Wertheimer 49-53.
[49] Beinart 21-22.

of factors have led to an increase in the number of day schools.

Beginning in the 1960s, America's Jewish population became increasingly middle class. As the public schools deteriorated, particularly in the cities, concern grew about overcrowding, crime, and drug use.[50] Many parents, Jews and non-Jews alike, began to search for alternatives. In our prior chapter on Politics, we cited Marc Dollinger's thesis that American Jewish political action was motivated by self-interest, and that when self-interest came into conflict with liberalism, American Jews would choose the latter.[51] This analysis might also be found to be the case with public education. Forced busing changed the nature of the public schools. At the same time, as private and "prep" schools, which for many years had been restricted, began to desegregate, American Jews became more aware of the status inherent in attending these institutions and the potential for advancement that their prestige could bring. Although Jews were great believers in public education, many preferred to seek alternatives to actually having their children attend public schools.

Beginning in the 1970s, there was increasing concern about the effectiveness of "supplemental education."[52] Many Jews who came of age during that period did not have fond associations with Sunday school.[53] There was also concern that the graduates of such programs knew little more than how to get through their bar/bat mitzvah. They could not read Hebrew, and this made participation in religious ritual less inviting. Jeremy Rabkin states, "Certainly, the uninitiated (to Hebrew and synagogue ritual) find it hard to take and must remain, at best, spectators of a staged ceremony and not full participants in communal worship."[54]

There was also concern about Jewish intermarriage and assimilation. According to the highly publicized 1990 National Jewish Population Survey (NJPS), cited by Wertheimer, Beinart and Rabkin, more than half of all Jews who married from 1985 to

[50] Wertheimer 49-53.
[51] Marc Dollinger, *Quest for Inclusion: Jews and Liberalism in Modern America* (New Jersey: Princeton University Press, 2000).
[52] Wertheimer 49-53.
[53] Wertheimer 49-53.
[54] Rabkin 37-40.

1990 married gentiles. Subsequent research has shown that graduates of supplementary schools are more than twice as likely to marry outside their faith as graduates of full-time Jewish schools.[55] Though the validity of these findings is arguable, they have been nonetheless taken to heart and have spurred a crisis of conscience.[56] In Jack Wertheimer's *Commentary* essay, he cites recent research that lists further benefits to attending day school: "The alumni are far more likely than others to observe a range of rituals and holidays, to contribute to Israel. Most impressive, perhaps, is the finding that graduates of day schools are considerably more inclined to wed other Jews."[57] Another survey by Rimor & Katz, sponsored by the Avi Chai foundation, found that "79% of Jewish day school graduates married other Jews, compared with fewer than half of those who had only received Jewish instruction in after-school programs."[58] Rabkin argues that children who receive a Jewish education are not only more committed to religious practice but also more likely to play an active role in the Jewish community as adults.[59] Rabkin cites a survey by Stephen M. Cohen, who revisited the 1990 NJPS statistics and found that, among Jewish activities, "part-time school, youth group, adolescent Israel travel, each make partial contributions. Day schools, Orthodox or not, typically exert much greater impact."[60] In other words, supplemental Sunday and Hebrew schools were out, day schools were in.

Day Schools: A Historical Perspective

Day schools were developed in Europe in the 19th century. In this country, they were at first the province of the Orthodox,[61] for whom day school was a way to strike a balance between "the old world, where being Jewish was a matter of course, and the new world, where one had to learn to be Jewish along with one's other

---

[55] Jack Wertheimer, "Who's Afraid of Jewish Day Schools?", *Commentary* (New York: Dec 1999); Peter Beinart, "The Rise of Jewish Schools", *The Atlantic Monthly* (Boston: Oct. 1999); Jeremy Rabkin, "A Choice for the Chosen", *Policy Review* (Washington: Jan/Feb 1999).

[56] Bruce Phillips, "Intermarriage and Jewish Education: Is There a Connection?", *Journal of Jewish Education* 66.1-2 (2000): 54.

[57] Wertheimer 49-53.

[58] Rabkin 37-40.

[59] Rabkin 37-40.

[60] Rabkin 37-40.

[61] Wertheimer 49-53.

studies." [62]   Jonathan D. Sarna, Professor of American Jewish History, who also speaks on the tradition of conservatism in the United States, also gives a historical perspective on American Jewish education.[63]   Sarna relates that, in 1803, New York's sole Jewish congregation, Shearith Israel, established a free school named Polonies Talmud Torah.[64] Students received a secular education plus a modest Jewish education, as the popular belief was that being an American Jew meant having a common education with the Protestant and Catholic Americans.[65]   The school received state aid; at that time, there was no concern about any violation of church and state.[66] In 1825, as public education became the standard, New York cut off aid to religiously sponsored schools. As a result, two models emerged: the so-called Protestant and Catholic models of education.[67] Sarna states:

> The Protestant model held that morality, universal values and patriotism, civics and critical skills should be taught in state-funded public schools to a mixed body of religiously diverse students, leaving only the fine points of religious doctrine and practice to be mastered by members of each faith in separate denominationally sponsored supplemental schools. The Catholic model, by contrast, insisted that such public schools really preached Protestant values and that the only way to maintain a minority (dissenting) tradition was through a separate system of religious schooling, which they organized on the parish system.[68]

For approximately 50 years, a number of Jewish day schools operated on the parochial model in such locales as New York, Charleston, Cincinnati and Washington, D.C. However, by 1870, they had almost all closed, replaced by supplemental Sunday or Sabbath schools.[69] Sarna quotes Cincinnati Reform Rabbi Isaac

---

[62] Wertheimer 49-53.
[63] Jonathan D. Sarna, "American Jewish Education in Historical Perspective," *Journal of Jewish Education* 64.1-2 (1998): 8-21.
[64] Sarna 8.
[65] Sarna 10.
[66] Sarna 10.
[67] Sarna 11.
[68] Sarna 11.
[69] Sarna 11.

Meyer Wise's report to the U.S. commissioner of education in 1870, "that the education of the young is the business of the state and the religious instruction . . . is the duty of religious bodies. Neither should interfere with the other." The Protestant model had triumphed.

The public school system became the source of a common education by which Jews thought they would become better Americans and play on a level playing field with their Christian counterparts. At the same time, Sunday schools evolved in several significant ways. First, there was some debate as to who should control Sunday schools: individual synagogues, communities or particular religious or philosophical movements. Some believed that the schools should remain independent. This debate goes on to this day with supplemental and day schools run by every variety of Jewish practice and community organization, including independent and non-denominational schools and programs.[70] Second, Sarna notes that the new American Sunday or Sabbath schools drove out the *melamdim* (teachers) of old, first by employing women almost exclusively as Sunday school teachers, then later by requiring that teachers have knowledge of modern Hebrew.[71]

Modern Hebrew was the other great educational development of the early 20th century, fostering the "Hebrew in Hebrew" movement (or *ivrit be ivrit*).[72] At the turn of the century, the fear was that the new generation of immigrants' children would lose touch with their Judaism as they sank into the American melting pot.[73] Samson Benderly, among other Hebraists, believed that modern Hebrew would give all Jews a common education, much like the public school curricula.[74] As a result, the preeminent task of Sunday and supplemental schools became to teach Hebrew. Curricula followed, and after-school hours were spent in what came to be known as "Hebrew School." This movement, Sarna reports, lasted until the 1970s, when it suddenly expired.[75]

---

[70] Sarna 13.
[71] Sarna 14.
[72] Sarna 17.
[73] Sarna 15.
[74] Sarna 14.
[75] Sarna 18.

No one seems to know why, but it may have to do with the fact
that Americans, in general, have never been known for their
ability to speak foreign languages.[76]

Today, fears that we are losing a generation of Jews have made
educational reform a hot topic. Given the cyclical nature of assimilation and nationalism, we need to consider the
question: Are we learning from the past, or just repeating it?
During the second half of the 20th century, day schools have slowly
increased in number. By 1945, there were 69 Jewish day schools
in the United States, with an enrollment of 10,200
students.[77] By 1975, there were 425 Orthodox day schools,
serving 82,200 students. As of January 1990, there were,
according to Rabkin, 731.[78] Since the early 1960s, the number of
children attending supplementary schools has fallen by half, to
about 270,000, but the number of students attending full-time
Jewish schools has grown, as cited above, to 200,000.[79] Most
impressive is the growth of non-Orthodox Jewish day schools.
"In the 1990s alone, enrollment in Reform, Conservative and
interdenominational schools has increased by 20%." [80] The
number of students in these schools is thought to be 50,000.[81]

Originally, almost all Jewish day schools were Orthodox. In
1957, the Conservative synagogue movement encouraged the
creation of the Solomon Schechter schools.[82] In addition to the
Schechter schools, the Reform movement has encouraged the
proliferation of temple schools throughout the country. There is
also a network of some 80 "independent" schools not affiliated
with any synagogue or denomination.[83] One of these is the New
Jewish High School in Waltham, Massachusetts. As profiled in
The Atlantic Monthly, the New Jewish High School, or "New Jew"
as it is called, will graduate its first class next June.[84] Many of
the parents at New Jewish High School are not that observant.

[76] Sarna 18.
[77] Rabkin 37-40.
[78] Rabkin 37-40.
[79] Beinart 21-22.
[80] Wertheimer 49-53.
[81] Rabkin 37-40.
[82] Rabkin 37-40.
[83] Rabkin 37-40.
[84] Beinart 21-22.

Indeed, a 1995-96 study of Conservative parents with children in Jewish schools found that fewer than half kept kosher in their homes, and fewer than a quarter kept kosher outside them.[85] Beinart quotes Jennifer Miller, head of the Rashi School, a Boston-area Reform elementary and middle school founded in 1986, who estimates that "only 10% to 15% of parents with children at her school can read and comprehend Hebrew."[86] Yet such parents, Beinart concludes, by choosing Jewish schools, are preparing their children to lead more observant, less-assimilated lives than they do.[87]

Several reasons have been offered for this phenomenon. At the turn of the millennium, Americans are placing a greater emphasis on searching for a more spiritual life and looking for ways to better integrate spirituality into their lives.[88] We have witnessed on the political level in Election 2000 how presidential candidates Bush and Gore both made religion an issue and spoke extensively about God. Similarly, we have noted that a *Public Interest* survey indicated that, despite unprecedented prosperity, voters felt that they were in the midst of a "moral crisis."[89] Accordingly, parents — feeling spiritually empty or morally challenged — want their children to lead more spiritual lives. For some, the solution may be to send them to a school that provides those values for them. This interest in spirituality is part of a generational quest by baby boomers, as discussed in such works as Wade Roof Clark's *Spiritual Marketplace: Baby Boomers and the Remaking of American Religion* (1999).[90] Increased enrollment at day schools may also be seen as a response to baby boomers' fears of assimilation and intermarriage. This generation of baby boomer parents has been characterized as over-involved, overprotective and fearful. They may be looking to the day school as an institution to do the work of protecting their children for them.

---

[85] Beinart 21-22.
[86] Beinart 21-22.
[87] Beinart 21-22.
[88] Diana Yacobi, "Jewish Education at the Frontline: A New Vision for the Twenty First Century," *Journal of Jewish Education* 66.3 (2000/2001): 30.
[89] Gertrude Himmelfarb, "Religion in the 2000 Election" *Public Interest* (Washington, D.C.: Spring 2001).
[90] Yacobi 32.

Another argument is that Jews today may feel more comfortable having their children identified as Jews. The era of America as a melting pot is over. As Rabkin notes, "The public schools that trained earlier generations of American Jews were the expression of a different America." [91] In today's society, multiculturalism and ethnic pride rule the day. Rabkin quotes Nathan Glazer's *We Are All Multiculturalists Now*: "The victory of multiculturalism in the public schools of America [has been] complete." [92] Combined with a much reduced fear of anti-Semitism, Jews are no longer as concerned that sending their children to Jewish day schools will make them less American. As Beinart states: "Earlier generations of Jews, according to Eduardo Rauch of the Jewish Theological Seminary in New York, sent their children to public school not simply as a means of ascending into the middle class but as a show of national loyalty. Today, in contrast, parents are willing to consider Jewish schools in part because they no longer fear being viewed as outsiders." [93] They are free to be Jews, to get Jewish education at Jewish institutions without fear of being penalized, ostracized or denied advantage or admission to other institutions of higher learning, or in any manner denied any opportunity offered to any other American.

Finally, there may be a "value-added" explanation for the popularity of day schools that we can call the "Sy Syms Theory." Syms is the venerable East Coast discount retailer, whose motto was "An educated consumer is our best customer." Consider the following: Beginning in the late 1960s, Jewish parents found themselves in a dilemma. Public schools were deteriorating and they sought alternatives. [94] What were their choices? They could either move to another neighborhood where the public schools were still good or pay for private school. Those who chose the private school option then needed to decide on criteria with which to select schools. This is acknowledged by Jennifer Miller of Boston's Rashi school: "As the public schools have eroded," she

---

[91]   Rabkin 37-40.
[92]   Rabkin 37-40.
[93]   Beinart 21-22.
[94]   Beinart 21-22.

is quoted as saying, "we are no longer being compared so much to public schools as to other independents."[95]

Parents who send their children to private rather than public school have a reasonable expectation that their children will receive a better education, and do so in a safe environment. They may consider the potential social advancement and status of joining an "old boys' network" where "it's not what you know but who you know." There also may be the perception that certain private schools have a better record of sending their graduates to prestigious colleges. However, other parents may feel equally uncomfortable sending their children to a private school where, in fact, their children are a minority. It is for these parents that the day schools offer "added value." Let us assume there exists a school — a Jewish day school. Assume it adheres to a brand of Judaism with which the parents are comfortable – Orthodox, Conservative, Reform or non-denominational. Assume it will be attended by children with parents of the same socioeconomic background and ethnic status. Assume that these schools are just as successful as the private schools at matriculating their students into colleges and universities. They cost about the same as private schools. So far, so good. However, here is the bonus: The children will learn more than children at other schools will. They'll learn Hebrew, religious practice and Jewish history. This is added value. Put these all together, and it is not difficult to understand the growth and success of such schools.

Many of these day schools have become very academically competitive and have been praised for the academic success of their graduates. Some are now difficult to gain admittance to. Among the many prestigious day schools are the Orthodox schools Ramaz in Manhattan and the Flatbush Yeshiva in Queens, the Conservative Solomon Schechter Schools and Reform institutions such as the Stephen Wise Temple and the Wilshire Boulevard Temple School, both in Los Angeles.[96]

---

[95] Beinart 21-22.
[96] Wertheimer 49-53.

Intermarriage and Jewish Education

Ever since the 1990 National Jewish Population Survey (NJPS) was used by two teams of researchers to conclude that the day school was either the only way or the most effective way to "inoculate" against intermarriage, day schools have been opening almost as fast as Starbucks. Consequently, Jewish education has become the focus of intense study and philanthropy. While those studies are meaningful, and there is no question of the success of Jewish day schools in promoting Jewish values, further research raises some important questions. Although the notion that the nature of Jewish education dictates the rate of intermarriage has become widely accepted as gospel, Bruce Phillips, a professor at the Hebrew Union College in Los Angeles, has reexamined the data. His positions pose alternatives to this premise and generate new ideas about how best to thwart intermarriage and ensure Jewish continuity.[97]

Phillips realized that adding the additional variables of Jewish parentage and generation make a substantial difference in interpreting the NJPS findings.[98] If one reasseses the data with the added variable of whether the parents are both Jewish-born or themselves intermarried, the pattern shifts. Statistics reveal that children of intermarried couples are more likely to intermarry than the norm.[99] Phillips suggests that it is also significant to consider Jewish parentage, because the study reveals that the level of education among children of mixed parentage is lower than that of the respondents with Jewish parentage.[100] Also relevant to this discussion is Judith Harris' *The Nurture Assumption*, one of the most controversial and attention-getting studies of recent years. Its provocative notion, expressed in its subtitle, asked "Do Parents Matter?" Her thesis, written and researched outside the academic world, was that children were most strongly influenced by their peer groups, and that what we attribute to "parenting" per se can be explained by the genetic heritage that

---

[97] Phillips 54.
[98] Phillips 54.
[99] Phillips 57.
[100] Phillips 57.

each child bears from their parents, not by their parents' influence. Similarly, here we might argue that there is a certain logical consistency to the premise that children of intermarried couples are more likely to intermarry themselves. We need not blame Sunday or Hebrew school or Hollywood.

As Phillips states, "When intermarriage and Jewish education are examined controlling for Jewish parentage, the impact of Jewish education is reduced. Endogamy rates among respondents with two Jewish parents do not vary much among the different types of Jewish education they received."[101] Phillips goes on to assess the importance of how many generations a respondent has been living in the United States (Phillips calls this factor "generation"), as applied to the studies that used the NJPS statistics. Again his findings are telling: "The association between generation and intermarriage is not unique to Jews."[102] By the third generation, intermarriage is rife, as studies have shown regarding Mexican-Americans, Catholics and Japanese-Americans.[103] When one controls for generation in the studies that run the duration and intensity of Jewish education against intermarriage, "the association between day school and intermarriage is greatly weakened."[104] Again, it is not the fault of supplemental education that intermarriage occurred (or conversely, we cannot credit day schools when Jews intermarry). Rather, intermarriage is a consequence of being a part of a culture for several generations. Phillips goes on to say that, if one takes into account both generation and parentage, almost all of the day school effect is accounted for.[105]

Having shown that, in fact, the glass is half-full, not half-empty, Phillips poses another question: What distinguishes those Jews who intermarried from those who did not? Phillips suggests another original analysis: Rather than look to what kind of Jewish education the respondents received, why not look at how many years of education they received and whether they

---

[101] Phillips 58.
[102] Phillips 59.
[103] Phillips 60.
[104] Phillips 60.
[105] Phillips 61.

received any informal Jewish education (such as a teen trip to Israel, Jewish content camping or a Jewish youth group)? Phillips discovered that respondents who ended their Jewish education at their bar mitzvah, and who had little or no continuing informal Jewish education in their teen years, were most likely to intermarry. Again using Judith Harris' work, we can postulate that having a non-Jewish peer group makes one more likely to date and marry non-Jews. It is possible that day school itself is responsible for a lower rate of intermarriage. It is the Jewish peer group that day schools provide that is so important. Significant Jewish involvement, whether from organized or informal sources, would be equally effective. Phillips suggests that we appropriate a different model and consider our Jewish teens as "at-risk youth." Like the youth groups who, at the turn of the last century, kept Jews out of gangs and crime, Phillips suggests we create a new generation of youth groups to keep our current generation out of new trouble: intermarriage.[106]

Jewish day schools are a valuable resource for reinforcing our ethnic and religious identity and keeping our children within the fold, but new developments imply that we must go further than day schools alone. These new ideas and approaches posited by Phillips indicate that it is also important to seek other, innovative solutions to improve supplemental education and target the majority of American Jewish children who still attend public schools.

Jewish Education in the 21ˢᵗ Century

Diana Yacobi, educational director of the Jewish Community Center of Fort Lee, delivered the keynote speech on supplementary education at the CAJE 2000 Annual Conference, articulating her vision for the 21ˢᵗ century. Yacobi suggests acknowledging and embracing those characteristics of supplemental education that make it distinctive. "The essential purpose of these forms of education is outreach and identity development, with educational goals centered in building literacy,

---

[106] Phillips 65.

fellowship, socialization, skills and experiences for Jewish life rather than scholarship or academic outcomes." [107]

Part of the task is to acknowledge the times in which we live. Yacobi cites Bethamie Horowitz's study, *Connections and Journeys: Assessing Critical Opportunities of Enhancing Jewish Identity*, as providing new insights. One of the major shifts that Horowitz sees is that if the first half of the century centered on a stance of acceptance versus rejection, the end of the century is characterized by personal choices about the levels of commitment to and engagement with Judaism. [108] What Yacobi recommends could strike some as revolutionary: She suggests that, "we leave behind the rigid mindset of assimilated versus observant Jews, and begin to view Jewish identity as shades of a rainbow, an ongoing process that unfolds over a lifetime. The door is always open, the possibilities endless." [109] Supplemental schools and programs are by their very nature free to adapt to contemporary realities. However, supplemental education cannot be curriculum driven alone. Yacobi acknowledges that part of the question is how to be better Jewish educators. [110] She suggests that attention be given to the types of preparation that serve as the foundation for a career in supplemental education. [111] Yacobi challenges her fellow educators to begin the new century by re-imagining supplementary education and creating a new professional stance to do so. It is no easy task, she admits, but Yacobi urges her fellow educators to begin that process. [112]

Armed with this new information, the issues and assumptions touched on at the start of this chapter are now turned on their head. As Wertheimer and Rabkin made clear, most of the major Jewish institutions and organizations are not in favor of school vouchers. We have discussed the reasons that Wertheimer and Rabkin have put forward and their answers to these objections. There may be other reasons that American Jews have

---

[107] Yacobi 30.
[108] Yacobi 32.
[109] Yacobi 33.
[110] Yacobi 35.
[111] Yacobi 36.
[112] Yacobi 39.

not supported the issue of school vouchers. The reasons, for example, may be political in nature; many American Jews still hew to liberal values, and many feel that a commitment to social action is part of how they express their Judaism. Even if their children attend private school, American Jews will not stop supporting public education. Returning to Mark Dollinger's theory that Jews act politically out of self-interest, we may also ask: Who stands to benefit in the school voucher argument? One could argue that Jewish parents who choose not to send their children to public school would benefit, whether they send their children to private schools or Jewish day schools. However, those parents do not represent the majority of Jews. The majority still send their children to public school and provide Jewish instruction for their children through supplemental education. Therefore, it should come as no surprise that, because most parents do not use Jewish day schools, the majority would not support legislation that would effectively have the taxpayers who do not use the service subsidize it not only for a minority of Jews but also for the variety of other faiths and organizations who would seek out such vouchers.

To keep matters in perspective, let us review certain facts. As stated above, although day school attendance has increased substantially, the great majority of American Jews still use "supplemental education." Jewish attendance in supplemental education programs may have decreased to 270,000, but this is still a significantly larger group than the 200,000 Jewish day school students. Similarly, although Jewish attendance in public schools has decreased from 95% in 1962, it still hovers at an overwhelming 65%, meaning that that great majority of American Jewish children attend public schools.

Finally, let us keep in mind that Jewish day schools, while an effective source of Jewish education, are not the only solution to problems affecting the American Jewish community. The facts of intermarriage and assimilation have beset Jewish communities since biblical times. A century ago, the fear that immigrant children would be absorbed into the melting pot and lose their Jewish identity was the cause for the creation of supplemental

Sunday school education and, following that, Hebrew School. Although intermarriage and assimilation pose real threats to Jewish identity and continuity, Yacobi argues that any possible solution must be tailored to our times and our realities and not motivated by fear. As Bruce Phillips suggests, we need to pay attention to our "at-risk youth" and find ways to engage them throughout high school in formal and informal Jewish education and surround them with Jewish peer groups with whom they will associate and perhaps, as their parents hope, one day in-marry. To that end, supplemental education needs to embrace its unique characteristics to improve its curricula and better its teachers for the 21st century. In the words of Diana Yacobi: "Let's begin."

Chapter Five

IMAGE:
Jewish Self-Image in Contemporary America

I saiah Berlin once wrote an essay observing that Jews — the essential and historical outsiders — spent so much time interpreting the various cultures in which they found themselves, they could never make contributions to such cultures themselves.[1] Over the course of our survey, we have found many examples to the contrary. As we have seen, Jewish contributions to culture, particularly in America, are extensive and substantial. The common thread in all these chapters is a recognition that we are in a time of pluralistic Judaism, a time when it is acceptable to turn inward and focus more on being Jewish, without the stigma that doing so makes us any less American.

Accordingly, we turn our attention to these last questions: Where do we, as American Jews, view ourselves in relation to

---

[1]   Brian Glanville, "What Is Jewish Culture?" *The Jewish Quarterly* 47.4 (2000-01): 39.

the rest of society? Who are those American Jews who are exploring, defining and presenting to the rest of society an image of Jewishness? What can we learn from them about the Jewish role in American society and the American role in Jewish society?

In this chapter, we find that American society is presented with a more complex, deeper portrait of American Jews. Rather than charting the progress of Jewish Americans up the social ladder and chronicling their adventures among the non-Jewish world, today's writers are inviting the non-Jewish world to view the dilemmas in our own insular communities. The voices are as varied as the experiences of American Jews. Jewish American writers reflect this diversity by their choice of subject material. The novels discussed in this chapter range from biblical narratives to multi-generational sagas, from novels chronicling the experience of assimilated Jews to that of the ultra-Orthodox. We are hearing increasingly from women, gays and lesbians and children of Holocaust survivors. Most often the narrator is an outsider observing an insular Jewish community. Their novels take place not just in New York or Chicago, but also in the shtetls of Europe and American ghettos, Israel and places as diverse as Hawaii and Brooklyn — wherever this new generation of writers imagine Jewish life. In this chapter we survey this explosion of new Jewish writing and review it in the context of the evolving self-image of Jews in contemporary American society.

American Jews Who Write and Jewish Writers

Embedded in our discussion of the Jewish role in America's image of Jews is the question: "Who is or what makes a Jew?" There is a distinction to be made between writers who are Jewish and writers who write Jewish. Isaac Bashevis Singer, in part because he wrote in Yiddish and Hebrew, felt he qualified as a Jewish writer more than most Americans.[2] By contrast, Norman Mailer, although born Jewish, has little Jewish content in his writing. Arthur Miller and Woody Allen rarely write about

---

[2] Glanville 39.

Jewish subjects, according to Anne Roiphe.[3] Is Singer someone
who writes Jewish, while Mailer is a Jewish writer who does not?
An amusing article in *Moment* asks the question, "Is Woody
Jewish?" The article goes on to distinguish between Woody Allen's
Jewish persona on film and his own personal life and the content
of his films, which are, in fact, not very concerned with Judaism
or Jewishness.[4] Similarly, David Leavitt, perhaps the most
prominent young gay Jewish writer, is also not usually
regarded as a Jewish writer. When it comes to Jewish
self-image, one could even ask: Who are we to say who's Jewish
and who's not? John Updike, who is not Jewish, has written a
successful series of novels about a Jewish writer named Bech. At
the same time, some writers who are perceived as non-Jewish
may in fact be more Jewish than we know. Mona Simpson, for
example, the author of many novels and short stories, including
Anywhere but Here, is perceived as a non-Jew; however, in her
personal life, she is married to a Jewish writer and raises her
children as Jews. So how do we make these distinctions?

Even among Jews, the distinctions are not clear. Few critics
or scholars seem to consider Michael Chabon as a "Jewish writer."
Yet his debut novel, *The Mysteries of Pittsburgh,* and his most
recent work, *The Adventures of Kavalier and Clay,* both feature
Jewish protagonists. *The Adventures of Kavalier and Clay,* which
won the Pulitzer Prize, is an ambitious work that deals with how
two young Jews — one a Holocaust refugee, the other American
born — transmute their fantasies into comic books. Chabon's
concerns and the novel's appeal are universal, but there is no
denying the Jewish content. So what then defines Jewish
writing? Is it the measure of success (or the lack thereof)? Not
really. Some Jewish novels have been very successful. For
example, Anita Diamant's *The Red Tent* has sold more than
350,000 copies. Clearly, there is no precise definition for a
Jewish writer or a Jewish novel. Instead, in this chapter we will
highlight a number of works by American Jews to see how they
express their self-image in contemporary society. To investigate

[3] Anne Roiphe, "From Jewish Writing to Writing Jewish," *Moment* Dec. 1999: 50-53.
[4] David Hozel, "Is Woody Jewish?" *Moment* Dec. 1999: 54-59.

and assess this issue, we will turn to a number of writers and creative artists who present an altogether different portrait of American Jews than has been offered in the past.

American Jews' Status as 'Outsider': A New 'Other'

In a recent issue of *Tikkun*, Sanford Pinsker wrote, "American Jews are no longer the American Other."[5] What Pinsker is referring to is the American Jew's status as outsider in American culture. As Pinsker sees it, it is our roles as outsiders (or our feelings as outsiders) that give American Jews something about which to write. Pinsker finds that being on the margin gives American Jews the critical vision to argue both from the left, like the Depression-era intellectuals, or from the right, like the *Partisan Review* crowd.[6] Today, however, American Jews have so completely assimilated that he wonders whether they haven't disappeared completely.[7]

Mark Shechner shares this view in an essay, "Is It Picasso or Is It the Jews?"[8] Shechner writes about the irrelevance of American Jewish fiction as follows: "In the academy as in the anthology, the Jewish writer is about as much in demand as Latin Vulgate homilies of the 10th century, a situation, it appears, of paradox. For, despite a rich, varied and voluminous fiction, Jewish writers in America, as anything like a 'camp' or a 'movement,' are virtually invisible. If literature is a talent show, Jewish writers fail to move the applause meter. It certainly feels as though Jews are in the shadow and that the limelight has moved on."[9]

The argument regarding the disappearance of American Jewish literature is generally formulated as follows: In the 1950s and 1960s, there was a vibrant and growing body of work by and about American Jews. These texts were mostly written by children of immigrants. This first generation of Americans sought refuge in literature from their parents' rough and tumble world. They were "smart" kids — college graduates for the most part —

---

[5] Sanford Pinsker, "Thinking About What the 'Other' Was, and Now Is," *Tikkun* 16.1 (2001): 51.
[6] Pinsker 51.
[7] Pinsker 51.
[8] Mark Shechner, "Is It Picasso or Is It the Jews?" *Tikkun* 16.1 (2001): 58-62.
[9] Shechner 53.

and they wrote about the ripples of negotiating the American world.[10] Probably no first sentence of a novel ever said it better than Saul Bellow's simple declaration in *The Adventures of Augie March*, "I am an American, Chicago born...." That opening was the clarion call.

Saul Bellow, Bernard Malamud and Philip Roth were the troika that drove this American Jewish fiction. Their novels were rich, varied and exciting, and they included such works as Malamud's *The Fixer* and Roth's *Portnoy's Complaint*. There were others, such as Norman Mailer and Joseph Heller, who were Jewish but found their way onto different subject matter because they didn't write about the American Jewish experience. Their books were not how the rest of America learned about contemporary American Jewish life. However, the consensus is that by the 1980s, the troika had so successfully passed into the pantheon that they had accomplished their task: They were part of American literature, and it seemed as if no one was left to follow. As Pinsker would put it, American Jews had so successfully assimilated that they put themselves out of business. According to Pinsker, American Jews have today become so much a part of the establishment, they are now the envy of other minorities. By way of example, Pinsker cites Gish Jen's novel *Mona in the Promised Land* (1996), in which the main character Mona Chang grows up in Scarsdale, wishing she were Mona Changowitz to fit in with the popular kids in high school; she decides to convert to Judaism.[11] American Jews were no longer "the other," or so it seemed.

Roth addresses this dilemma in his recent novel *The Human Stain*, in which he turns the notions of ethnic identity inside out.[12] In *The Human Stain*, Professor Coleman Silk of Athena College is let go after he refers to two African-American students who never seem to attend his class as "spooks." Silk's supporters find the charges of racism against him equally ironic and absurd; as a Jew, he had to endure much prejudice to become head of the

---

[10] Roiphe 51-80.
[11] Roiphe 52.
[12] Roiphe 52.

classics department. The twist here is that rather than being a Jewish intellectual patriarch, Silk is actually a product of the African-American-dominant area of Newark in which he lived. When given the opportunity, Silk decided to leave his past and his race behind.[13] He transcended his roots so well that he is a victim of a politically correct witch-hunt. The point is that it is no longer enough to be a Jew to get a rise out of Roth: you have to be a black man pretending to be a Jew. For American Jews, writes Pinsker, the question remains: Are we no longer "the Other", or is there a "human stain" that won't leave us?[14]

In truth, critics have been mourning the death of Jewish American literature for more than three decades. As Andrew Furman points out in "The Exaggerated Demise of the Jewish-American Writer," critic Irving Howe sounded the first death knell in his 1977 introduction to the anthology *Jewish American Stories* when he observed, "American Jewish fiction has probably moved past its high point."[15]

Now, as we begin a new century and a new millennium, a whole new generation of writers has had to reinvent themselves in the absence of being the American Other. As Furman notes, "Irving Howe never anticipated the emergence of new, distinctively Jewish-American sensibilities."[16] As we will see, a number of American Jews have found a way to portray "the Other" within the American Jewish community. "Whatever else America may be," writes Pinsker, "it is a place where people are constantly reinventing themselves."[17] Or, as Morris Dickstein has commented, "The current resurgence of Jewish-American writing in a world rife with assimilation is as surprising as the survival of the Jews themselves."[18] Dickstein credits the new religious currents that sprung up in America following Israel's Six-Day War in 1967, such as the Havurah movement, with reinvigorating a new generation, particularly women, with

---

[13] Roiphe 52.
[14] Roiphe 52.
[15] Andrew Furman, "The Exaggerated Demise of the Jewish-American Writer" *The Chronicle of Higher Education* [Washington] 6 July 2001: B7-9
[16] Furman B7-9.
[17] Roiphe 52.
[18] Morris Dickstein, "Ghost Stories: The New Wave of Jewish Writing," *Tikkun* (Nov/Dec 1997): 1-10.

emotional and spiritual intensity. "The new Jewish emphasis on identity," writes Dickstein, "the revival of interest in Jewish history, Jewish festivals and sacred Jewish texts could not help but lead to a new Jewish writing." [19]

Susanne Klingenstein of the Massachusetts Institute of Technology identifies six different marginal worlds that now serve as "sources of creative inspiration and Jewish authenticity." They are the shtetl, Israel, Orthodox and Hasidic communities, Holocaust survivors, gays and immigrants.[20] At the same time, scholars and critics have identified several themes that emerge in writing about these groups, most notably the tension between the religious Jew in the secular world and the secular Jew in opposition to the religious world.[21] Just as our chapter on Politics explained how one's stance toward the Jewish religion can inform one's political stance, the image of American Jews today is informed not so much by their relation to other non-Jews as it is by their relation to other Jews. By discussing the works that fall into these categories, we will see how the image of American Jews has expanded and deepened.

Another Kind of Jewish Voice

"What is so striking about the current crop of American Jewish writers," author Anne Roiphe remarks, "is that, unlike the prior generation, they are not hurtling toward assimilation." [22] Citing such writers as Allegra Goodman, Aryeh Lev Stollman, Pearl Abraham, Ehud Havazelet, Daphne Merkin, Natan Englander and Leon Wieseltier, Roiphe sees a new landscape: "What we see is another kind of Jewish voice. This one was raised within the Jewish tradition, and although it has serious objections to how it was informed, it does not mumble out of a Jewish vacuum." [23]

What impresses Roiphe most is the ability of a new

---

[19] Dickstein 1-10.

[20] Susanne Klingenstein, "Jewish American Fiction, Act III: Eccentric Sources of Inspiration: The Ties That Bind," *After Twenty-Five Years, a Look Back and Ahead: Studies in American Jewish Literature*, Daniel Walden, ed., 18 (1999): 83.

[21] Rahel Musleah, "Finding Our Voice: Jewish Women Take the Literary World by Storm," *Jewish Woman* (2000): 18-19.

[22] Musleah 52.

[23] Musleah 52.

generation to be as comfortable with Jewish literacy as with American literature, and to blend both worlds in one work.[24] As an example, Roiphe hails Leon Wieseltier's *Kaddish* as a major accomplishment.[25] *Kaddish*, says Roiphe, "[is] a passionate portrait of a man in grief, an American Jewish man who has rejected his father's ways but not forgotten them. Wieseltier has created a major work that hooks the laws of the rabbis to the modern soul, that post-Freudian, American choices-abound, free-to-leave soul. I take the publication of *Kaddish* as a sign that Jewish culture in America will now turn toward itself, not by going backward, not by engaging in ancestor worship or repetition, but by going forward into new creative paths that nevertheless have continuity with the most exciting parts of our history." [26] In a similar fashion, we might also hail Jonathan Rosen's meditation *The Talmud and the Internet*, which traces the author's personal connections between text and hyperlink in his grandmother's generation and his own life.[27] Both works received strong praise in the mainstream, non-Jewish press, in such forums as the *New York Times* and the *Los Angeles Times*.

Roiphe came of age at a time when the premier Jewish voices were primarily male. As in the areas of politics and philanthropy, Jewish women, until very recently, were denied the attention they deserved. Just as women's organizations are now gaining recognition for their political work and breaking through in established philanthropy and/or establishing their own foundations, so too in literature Jewish women are now important voices to reckon with.

Beyond Ethnic Stereotypes:
A Woman's Voice in American Jewish Literature

Jewish women have, in the past, been the objects of ethnic stereotyping.[28] The most obvious example is the Jewish American Princess, or JAP, which was a prominent character for

---

[24] Roiphe 51.
[25] Roiphe 53.
[26] Roiphe 79.
[27] Jonathan Rosen, *The Talmud and the Internet* (New York: Farrar, Straus and Giroux, 2000).
[28] Anna Petrov Bumble, "The Intellectual Jewish Woman Versus the JAP in the Worlds of American Jewish Writers," *Studies in American Jewish Literature*, Vol. 19 (2000): 26.

many years in American popular culture. Her lineage can be traced back to Herman Wouk's *Marjorie Morningstar,* and is frozen in the culture by Philip Roth's *Goodbye Columbus.*[29] For many years afterward, the JAP was a stereotypical character in books, TV shows and movies such as *Private Benjamin*. By the 1970s, Jewish women struck back, creating their own stereotype: the intellectual girl, found in the work of Cynthia Ozick and, more recently, in the work of Rebecca Goldstein. The smart, sexy (or promiscuous) version is Isadora Wing in Erica Jong's classic *Fear of Flying*.

Although this chapter does not focus on gender issues, we are interested in the images by which Jews are defined for the American public. Michele Aaron has written a provocative essay, "The Queer Jew and Cinema: From Yidl to Yentl and Back and Beyond," which examines images of Jews as women in America.[30] In her essay, Aaron confounds the definitions of male, female, straight and gay in American culture to show how Jews have been denigrated in the past and how, in two examples, women have sought to redress the situation. Aaron argues that the films *Yidl Mitn Fildl*, the classic 1936 Molly Picon movie, and the 1983 Barbara Streisand film *Yentl* deconstruct anti-Semitic stereotypes and — in ways appropriate to the times in which each was made — empower their Jewish heroines. Aaron's argument, in brief, is that in order to portray Jews as weak, society has depicted them as effeminate or gay. Streisand and Picon, each in her own way, sought to show Jews and women as empowered by playing with that stereotype in stories where a woman poses as a man. In both cases, they emerge victorious: *Yidl* ends with Picon sailing to America for a singing tour, and *Yentl* with Streisand immigrating to America, where she will be free to continue her studies. In these works, Streisand and Picon redefine Jewish identity for American audiences.

Today, several young Jewish women are redefining the image of Jews and Jewish women in particular in their writing. As Musleah points out in "Finding Our Voice: Jewish Women

[29] Bumble 26
[30] Michele Aaron, "The Queer Jew and Cinema: From Yidl to Yentl and Back and Beyond," *Jewish Culture and History* 3.1 (Summer 2000): 23-44.

Take the Literary World by Storm," there are a number of outstanding new female Jewish writers on the scene. These include, among many others, Nomi Eve, Myla Goldberg, Anita Diamant, Simone Zeilitch and Kate Singer.[31] These writers' subject matters, while diverse, are focused on the Jewish experience. For example, Eve is the author of *The Family Orchard*, the story of six generations in a Jewish family. In this saga, which grew out of Eve's father's journals, she creates a tale that alternates between her father's factual descriptions and her own fictionalized ones. At the other end of the spectrum, Goldberg's *Bee Season* tells an insular tale of an 11-year-old spelling bee champion who is coached by her father, a Reconstructionist cantor.[32] As is the case with so many con-temporary Jewish authors, the appeal of these writers extends far beyond a Jewish audience. For example, Tova Mirvis wrote *The Ladies Auxiliary,* a novel about an outsider in Memphis' Orthodox community. Mirvis says that Asian-Americans and Methodists alike feel the book speaks to them.[33] Diamant's retelling of the biblical story of Dinah in *The Red Tent* has been translated into 14 languages.[34] These books have met with both critical and popular success, receiving multiple print-ings in hardcover and then in paperback.[35] For these women, literary agent Gail Hochman says three themes predominate: "the legacy of the Holocaust, survival in Israel and living in the world as a secular Jew." [36]

Subject Matters

Contemporary American Jewish writers are presenting a different face to the world in more ways than one. As noted above, in "Jewish American Fiction, Act III: Eccentric Sources of Inspi-ration," Susanne Klingenstein argues that the different worlds that contemporary Jews travel in serve as "sources of creative

---

[31] Musleah 16.
[32] Musleah 16.
[33] Musleah 19.
[34] Musleah 16.
[35] Musleah 16.
[36] Musleah 18-19.

inspiration and Jewish authenticity." She lists six different slices of American Jewish life as current themes: the gay community, the Holocaust, Israel, shtetl life, Orthodox and Hasidic communities and immigrants.[37] While this list is intentionally definitive, examining each of these categories leads to a better understanding of how American Jews have come to inhabit each of these landscapes. However, it is important to note that the boundaries are by no means clear. The novels cited by critics as "gay" in theme also have characters who are children of Holocaust survivors; the novels written about Israel feature immigrants or explore the Orthodox world. Each segment tells its own story, but they merge to paint a picture of America and of American Jews in the 21st century.

Subsets and Similarities: Jewish and Gay

The first generation of American Jewish literature was male-dominated and defiantly heterosexual. These new American Jews were adventurers seeking pleasure with women, Jewish and non-Jewish. The vanishing point may well have been Philip Roth's *Portnoy's Complaint*, a novel that took heterosexual self-indulgence to its extreme. After *Portnoy*, what else was there to say? Gays and lesbians were not part of this new Jewish identity; it was up to gay individuals to present their own story and argue that they had a place in American Jews' self-definition. Some critics argue that, as Jews felt more comfortable in the mainstream, they were (and are) able to reveal themselves as they truly are. In essence, they have been able to come out of the closet. Accordingly, a number of Jewish novels in which the protagonists are also gay have started to appear. At the same time, a number of critics sought to equate the status in society of gays with that of American Jews. In America, until recently, one would be hard pressed to think of pioneering American Jewish gay novelists, even closeted ones. Even today, David Leavitt, one of the better-known writers on gay themes,

---

[37] Klingenstein 83.

has little Jewish content to his work.[38]   However, as the gay liberation movement came of age, many Jews were involved at the forefront of that battle.   As a result, we began to have images of Jewish gays and lesbians.   In this respect, Larry Kramer's 1978 novel *Faggots* can be seen as a milestone.

Kramer was one of the best-known gay activists of the 1980s. As Michael Weingrad makes clear in "The Jewish Contexts of Larry Kramer's *Faggots*," Kramer has always been vocal about the connection between his Judaism and his homosexuality.[39] Kramer underscored this analogy by titling his 1994 collection of speeches and essays on the AIDS epidemic, "Reports From the Holocaust."[40]   As Weingrad notes, "In *Faggots,* we see that Kramer's vision of gay politics and his excoriations of the community when it fails to conform to this vision are both products of a particularly Jewish imagination."[41]

Weingrad believes that there is a thesis implicit in the novel that this new waking gay community parallels the development of the Jewish immigrant community at the beginning of the 20th century.[42]   As Weingrad puts it, the gay community, like the Jewish one, is "a suspect group, apart from the mainstream, yet one that is now feeling its own sense of self, and therefore becoming cognizant of its decisive impact upon the definitions of American-ness itself.   It is, after all, a ghetto novel, therefore finding itself in a tradition of ethnic writing."[43]   In one particularly memorable passage, Kramer spoofs Gershon Sholem's famous essay "Towards an Understanding of the Messianic Idea in Judaism."[44]   What, for Sholem, is an argument for Jewish rejection of assimilation becomes a cry from Kramer for gays to come out of the closet.   In essence, Kramer is arguing that gays should form their own "Zionist" movement.[45]   Most interesting is Kramer's critical stance toward the gay community itself, which parallels the stance that authors such as

---

[38] Klingenstein 84.
[39] Michael Weingrad, "The Jewish Contexts of Larry Kramer's *Faggots*" *Response* Fall 1999: 86.
[40] Weingrad 86.
[41] Weingrad 86-87.
[42] Weingrad 89.
[43] Weingrad 89.
[44] Weingrad 91-92.
[45] Weingrad 92.

Bellow and Roth have taken toward their fellow Jews. Kramer is an activist, and to Kraemer and Weingrad, that is because he is Jewish.

Weingrad is not alone in seeing a connection between Jews and gays. For her part, Klingenstein posits the affinity between Jews and gays as a common history of "stereotyping, marginalization, repression, persecution."[46] These conflicts are seen as prime sources of fiction and of self-definition. Among the works that Klingenstein cites is Michael Lowenthal's *The Same Embrace* (1998), in which two twin brothers are equally ostracized by their assimilated parents, one because he is gay, the other because he is Orthodox.[47] In the novel, reconciliation only becomes possible after their beloved grandmother who fled the Holocaust falls into a coma, precipitating a crisis that exposes family secrets.[48] In the *New York Times*, Linda Barrett Osborne described *The Same Embrace* as "an eloquent exploration of the nature of human faith, the consequences of judgment and the stubborn endurance of family ties."[49] Yet the context of these conflicts is composed of the very elements that make up the mosaic of contemporary American Judaism: Orthodoxy, the impact of the Holocaust, identity and homosexuality.

In this respect, Lowenthal himself is a good example. Lowenthal's paternal grandfather was a rabbi who lost a son in Bergen-Belsen.[50] Lowenthal grew up in a religiously Conservative home, but he describes himself as assimilated: "I'm the greatest fear of the Jewish religious establishment," he says, ". . . the drifter."[51] But Lowenthal affirms that he is immersed in Jewish culture and being Jewish is part of his identity.[52] At the same time, he notes, that, like Jews, "gay people are also wrestling with [assimilation]. How do you do it without losing what's distinctive about your group?"[53]

[46] Klingenstein 83.
[47] Klingenstein 83.
[48] Linda Barrett Osborne, "Family Is Family, at First and at Last," *New York Times* 22 Nov. 1998.
[49] Osborne 22 Nov. 1998.
[50] Sarah Horowitz, "Novelist Examines Converging World of Jews and Gays," *Jewish Bulletin of Northern California* 23 Oct. 1998.
[51] Horowitz 23 Oct. 1998.
[52] Horowitz 23 Oct. 1998.
[53] Horowitz 23 Oct. 1998.

Lowenthal sees a definite connection between gays and Jews. For example, he says, "while Jews have often lived in actual ghettos, gays inhabit a metaphorical one.[54] Lowenthal observes there are concrete ways in which the experiences of being gay and Jewish are similar: "Growing up as a Jewish kid, you feel kind of queer and a little bit left out because you're not cele-brating the same holidays, but at the same time you feel kind of special. . . . You have your own kinds of foods and traditions and language. For gay people, the downside is much more heightened, but there is also a kind of special feeling, which is really the basis for the bond when gay people come out. It's the same kind of *mispoche* Jews feel in the temple."[55] Both Jews and gays are often discriminated against, Lowenthal believes, and also are often accused of wielding disproportionate power. Lowenthal has told a reporter that he believes that speaking about the unspeakable – both as a Jew and a gay man – is ultimately freeing.[56]

Roiphe also notes the important contribution that gay Jews are making. "We are also hearing from gay Jews who were raised within the tradition, and their work too is deeply Jewish but still deeply gay."[57] Roiphe cites the work of Aryeh Lev Stollman, author of *The Far Euphrates*, who Roiphe believes "may prove to be an artist of the first order."[58] *The Far Euphrates* is set in Windsor, Ontario, and tells the coming-of-age story of Alexander, a rabbi's son.[59] Alexander is surrounded by his mother, a Gypsy seer, a cantor and his wife, and the cantor's twin sister (the cantor and his sister were both part of Mengele's Auschwitz twin experiments). Everyone has their secrets, even Alexander, who we come to understand is gay. As Margot Livesey wrote in the *New York Times,* "Most novels would be content to show our lives are shaped by history, but this one seems after something larger. At the heart of *The Far Euphrates* lie the vexed questions raised

[54] Horowitz 23 Oct. 1998.
[55] Horowitz 23 Oct. 1998.
[56] Horowitz 23 Oct. 1998.
[57] Roiphe 52.
[58] Roiphe 52.
[59] Sarah Coleman, "Unusual Coming-of-Age Novel Rich in Jewish Knowledge, Lore," *Jewish Bulletin of Northern California* 7 Nov. 1997.

by the Holocaust and its legacy: how we try for ourselves to solve the riddle of God's existence and cultivate a sense of mercy in an unforgiving age."[60] Stollman is another writer who believes that his Jewishness influences his writing. Stollman, who is also a rabbi's son, has said that all of his work has a strong Jewish flavor, due in part to his classical Jewish education. He lists among his influences S.Y. Agnon,[61] in whose work Roiphe also sees parallels.[62] Interestingly enough, both Lowenthal and Stollman have novels that not only feature gay protagonists, but also use the Holocaust as a looming unspoken influence. This presence only highlights the role the Holocaust continues to play in American Jews' self-image.

The Holocaust and the Generations that Followed

Although most American Jews did not experience the Holocaust, and many were not directly touched by it, it continues to define their outlook. In some ways, this appropriation of the tragedy is part of Judaism. Literature on and of the Holocaust continues to grow to such an extent that Holocaust education is now part of the mainstream of American life. The importance of the Holocaust to mainstream American culture can be seen in Washington, D.C.'s monumental Holocaust Museum, which sits on the Mall, near other American institutions: the Smithsonian, the National Archives and the National Air and Space Museum. Most of what we know today of the Holocaust, as Americans, comes from the works of foreign-based fiction and nonfiction writers working in America. Although Elie Wiesel was born in Hungary, immigrated to Israel, and wrote his first novels in French in Paris before coming to America, his novels such as *Night* and *Dawn* are read in high schools and on college campuses all over America. Wiesel himself has lived in this country for several decades and taught a seminar for many years at Boston University. A generation of Americans, Jewish and non-Jewish, have been affected by his work.

[60] Margot Livesey, "In a World of Secrets," *New York Times* 21 Sept. 1997.
[61] Coleman 7 Nov. 1997.
[62] Roiphe 52.

Jerzy Kosinski, author of *The Painted Bird*, is another American Jewish writer who created memorable fiction set during the Holocaust. Although born in Poland, Kosinski immigrated to the United States and published his works here. *The Painted Bird* remains a classic work through which many first approach the horrors of the Holocaust. Kosinski's last novel, *The Hermit of 69ᵗʰ Street*, had among its many themes the subject of Holocaust denial.

The Holocaust has come to play a part in the imagination of American-born writers as well, some of whom are not even Jewish, most notably in the case of William Styron's *Sophie's Choice*. Matters are further complicated when one considers that *Schindler's List*, Australian author Thomas Keneally's novel about a Los Angeles-based Holocaust survivor's war-time rescue by a gentile, became an important film by American Jewish director Steven Spielberg.

Along with the increase of literary accounts of the Holocaust, historians have also made enormous efforts to record and publish Holocaust survivor memoirs. We will neither list nor discuss them in detail here. Let it suffice for our purposes to note that it would be hard for any American Jew, or for that matter any American, to have no perception of the Holocaust, or to have no association between the Jews and the Holocaust as part of his or her consciousness. Archives at Yale have recorded thousands of oral and video histories of Holocaust survivors. The Survivors of the Shoah Foundation have recorded more than 50,000 more Holocaust survivor interviews, digitizing and indexing the accounts to make them searchable and available for students and scholars.

For better or worse, the Holocaust has strongly marked the identities of American Jews. Therefore, it is no surprise that the legacy of the Holocaust has become a subject for discussion in a number of recent novels, in a variety of forms. Most notably, these works are now exploring a contemporary theme: the impact of the Holocaust on the children of the generation who survived the Shoah. Klingenstein cites three novels in particular — *Fugitive Pieces* by Anne Michaels (1997), *The Far Euphrates* (1997) and Melvin Jules Bukiet's *After* (1996) — as examples of this new form.[63]

Bukiet, the son of survivors, sets his novel, *After*, in Germany immediately following the war. The plot centers on a group of survivors who plan to steal an 18-ton cube of gold made by the Nazis from the dental fillings of murdered Jews.[64] Klingenstein describes Bukiet's work as angry and deeply comic, with anger directed not at the Nazis but "against a dead Jewish God." Bukiet's survivors are forgers, killers and sleazy hustlers looking for money, sex and revenge. This is not necessarily the best image of Jews, but that is the point: Bukiet wants to show that, post Holocaust, all bets are off. Klingenstein quotes Bukiet's protagonist as saying: "Did Jews survive? I don't know what a Jew is anymore. I don't think I bear any resemblance to my father or grandfather or some ancestor with camels. Things are different now."[65] Klingenstein argues that Bukiet's depiction of the survivors as criminals "appears to be Bukiet's revenge on the god who, for centuries, demanded obedience, self-discipline and moral rectitude from his people and then abandoned them to unspeakable horrors."[66]

Thane Rosenbaum is a child of Holocaust survivors whose collection of short stories *Elijah Visible* (1996) details children of survivors living with the pain they did not experience themselves.[67] In Klingenstein's estimation, Rosenbaum's work "is a self-propagating universe of terror and suffering." The work "[does] not point to a larger Jewish life beyond the pains of his generation. Moreover, they reduce the Jews, even those living in a peaceful, open society, once more to victims."[68] Rosenbaum's work is also the subject of analysis by Florida Atlantic University's Alan Berger.[69] In "Mourning, Rage and Redemption: Representing the Holocaust: The Work of Thane Rosenbaum," Berger argues that for Rosenbaum's second-generation characters, the Holocaust is a "central and unworked-through trauma; one in which mourning and rage

---

[63] Klingenstein 84.
[64] Klingenstein 84.
[65] Klingenstein 84.
[66] Klingenstein 84.
[67] Klingenstein 84.
[68] Klingenstein 84.
[69] Alan Berger, "Mourning, Rage and Redemption: Representing the Holocaust: The Work of Thane Rosenbaum," *Studies in American Jewish Literature*, Daniel Walden, ed., vol. 19 (2000): 7-51.

cripple the protagonists.[70]   In Berger's estimation, the task for
Rosenbaum's characters is to deal with a "Final Solution that ha[s]
no end" by working through their rage and mourning.[71] Berger's
view of Rosenbaum's work is more positive than Klingenstein's.
Berger believes that Rosenbaum's characters find healing in the
prayer for the dead, the Kaddish, which suggests a kinship with
generations of Jews that is greater than the Holocaust.[72]

In contrast, the characters in Anne Michaels' *Fugitive Pieces*
find their way to love and caring.[73] The plot of *Fugitive Pieces* is
as follows: Ben, the child of survivors, is a college professor who
is filled with fear. Ben discovers the poetry of Jakob Beer, a
Polish survivor who witnessed the murder of his family and then
fled to the forest where he was saved by a Greek archaeologist
named Athos. Athos taught Beer how to live again and, in turn,
Beer teaches Ben. As Klingenstein puts it, "the lineage of trauma
is balanced by a lineage of loving and caring." [74] Whether the
legacy is positive or negative for the generation that follows the
Holocaust is not as important as acknowledging its pervasive
quality. It is the Holocaust that shapes Bukiet's, Rosenbaum's
and Michaels' characters in present-day narrative and plays a
significant role in their self-definition as Jews.

Bukiet, who has taught at Sarah Lawrence College, finds the
influence of the Holocaust pervasive and has written on the
subject, most notably for a 1997 *Tikkun* Literary Symposium.[75]
Bukiet's essay "Machers and Mourners" essentially divides all of
American Jewish literature in the two categories of his title.[76]
Bukiet's argument is that Jewish history is an unrelenting tale of
"loss, torture, humiliation and atrocity;" however, Bukiet is not
bitter. As he writes: "Bitter, moi? How's bitterness possible when
the 'I can get it for you wholesale' slaughter of generations of
ancestors has given us the gift of the greatest subject in the world,
the same gift the snake gave Eve in Eden, knowledge of good and

[70] Berger 7-51.
[71] Berger 7-51.
[72] Berger 7-51.
[73] Klingenstein 84.
[74] Klingenstein 84.
[75] Melvin Jules Bukiet, "Machers and Mourners," *Tikkun* (1997): 1-10.
[76] Bukiet 1-10.

evil."[77] Apparently, Bukiet subscribes to S. J. Perelman's famous dictum that "misery breeds copy."[78] Or, as Bukiet puts it himself, "Human horror breeds literature."[79]

To this horror, Bukiet argues, there are two possible responses. One is the mourner's, whose authors "share one ultimate loss: None of them can produce a redemptive Jewish God who entails a viable rationale for Jewish existence."[80] The other is that of the macher, who "perceives the same void... and steps in."[81] The mourner experiences displacement from society, while the macher asserts himself and flies in the face of all convention. Bukiet goes on to break down all recent Jewish writers into one of the two categories. For example, Wiesel is a mourner, while Kosinski is a macher (in *The Painted Bird*, the boy gets vengeance by derailing a Polish train); Philip Roth is a macher, Malamud a mourner. Among contemporary Jewish writers, Bukiet finds Thane Rosenbaum, Aryeh Lev Stollman, Myra Goldberg, Jonathan Rosen and Tova Reich to be mourners, while Michael Chabon, Neil Gordon, Jonathan Levi and Francine Prose are machers.[82] Bukiet's point is that American Jewish literature may or may not die, but it will certainly go well recorded.[83] Equally important, these writers are examining how their interior landscape conforms not only to other Americans but to other Jews. Increasingly this is the subject matter of Jewish American fiction, an examination by one outsider of insular groups of American Jews living in their own community – whether it is the community of the religious or the assimilated.

Insider Views of the Orthodox and Hasidim

Americans and American Jews have become increasingly fascinated by the world of the Orthodox and the Hasidim. For many years, this literary landscape was primarily the province of

[77] Bukiet 1-10.
[78] S. J. Perelman, *Conversations with S. J. Perelman* (Jackson, Miss.: University of Mississippi Press, 1995).
[79] Bukiet 1-10.
[80] Bukiet 1-10.
[81] Bukiet 1-10.
[82] Bukiet 1-10.
[83] Bukiet 1-10.

Chaim Potok, who with *The Chosen* (1967) made this world accessible to Jews and non-Jews alike. Potok, who was raised in an Orthodox Jewish home, views much of mainstream America from a different vantage point than most American Jewish novelists of the same era.[84] "It might be argued," notes one critic, "that Potok starts from a strongly Jewish viewpoint and overlays this with a conception of American culture as the secular Other Side."[85] In Potok's novels, the two sides struggle (often within one individual such as his character Asher Lev).[86]

Daphne Merkin's *Enchantment* is another more recent benchmark.[87] Merkin, who specializes in "saying the unspeakable" in the most precise and luminous of prose, writes as a character who has left the Orthodox world yet remains tied to it. Merkin's collection of nonfiction essays and articles called *Dreaming of Hitler* is equally provocative.[88] Surveying the new generation of American Jewish writers, Anne Roiphe finds that "The Orthodox world is understood but not necessarily accepted."[89] Allegra Goodman's recent novel, *Katerskill Falls*, describes an observant woman's attempt to "carve out a niche of self-independence" within her tight-knit community, a summer resort in the Catskills.[90] Goodman began her career as a satirist, and she brings a bemused tone to her stories of contemporary American Jews.[91] Her first collection of stories, *The Family Markowitz*, chronicled three generations of a clan whose sense of Jewish identity is as quirky as their characters. Morris Dickstein describes her attitude toward secular Jews as "detached, amused and forgiving." As Dickstein sees it, "The foibles of intellectuals like Ed and Henry Markowitz – one a self-important strategic analyst, the other an aesthete of wavering sexual preference – belong to the ever-shifting human comedy rather than the

---

[84] Joanna Barkess, "Painting the Sitra Achra: Culture Confrontation in Chaim Potok's Asher Lev Novels," *The Resonance of Twoness: Ambivalent Faith in an Ambiguous World, Studies in American Jewish Literature* vol. 17 (1998): 17.
[85] Barkess 17.
[86] Barkess 17.
[87] Daphne Merkin, *Enchantment* (New York: Harcourt Brace, 1986).
[88] Daphne Merkin, *Dreaming of Hitler* (New York: Harcourt Trade, 1999).
[89] Roiphe 52.
[90] Klingenstein 83
[91] Klingenstein 83.

history of modern nihilism." [92] Goodman's latest novel, *Paradise Park*, describes one woman's two-decade quest for spiritual enlightenment.[93]

Another young author who writes of conflicts between the secular and observant worlds is Pearl Abraham. Abraham's debut novel *The Romance Reader* (1995) was set in the world of Brooklyn's Hasidim. It told the story of Rachel Benjamin, the eldest of seven siblings. Abraham portrays a world in which men toil or study, women stay home and are married by the time they reach 18 and have eight children before they are 30. In the novel the protagonist, Rachel, enters an arranged marriage but, as her world constricts, she flees to New York for a few days, returning to her family to get a proper divorce. In a similar vein, Abraham's second novel, *Giving Up America*, tells the tale of Deena, who chose a non-Hasidic husband and whose seven-year marriage is childless and falling apart. Although she argues against her father who predicted the union would not work, she ends up returning to him in Jerusalem; apparently, the freedom America offered did not satisfy her either. For writers such as Merkin, Goodman and Abraham, spiritual and emotional fulfillment is part of their quest as American Jews. In the process, they've revealed that the tension between various segments of the American Jewish community can be as rich a subject as assimilation once was. For some writers searching to explore insular communities of Jews, their imagination takes them far from the contemporary experience to Israel, to shtetls of old or to chronicle the experience of recent Jewish immigrants.

Israel in the Imagination of American Jews

Although American Jews strongly identify with Israel, it has played little part in their written self-explorations. Few American characters travel to Israel, and few Israeli characters appear in American Jewish works.[94] Klingenstein maintains that, when Israel has recently been used as a fictional device, it is as a

---

[92] Dickstein 1-10.
[93] Musleah 21.
[94] Klingenstein 83.

place where writers sent their protagonists in search of self-transformation.[95] "It is where you went to discover your Jewish self," Klingenstein writes. This is particularly true in two very different novels: Nessa Rapoport's *Preparing for Sabbath* and Philip Roth's *Operation Shylock*.

Preparing for Sabbath was written, in part, as a response to an image of American Jews as envisioned by the earlier works of Roth. Rapoport has described her writing of the novel as a "mission":

I had a passion to write a different kind of Jewish novel from the ones we had been reading, those by Bellow, Roth and Malamud portraying the seductive, glamorous non-Jewish America. I was interested in a story that hadn't been told, that of a young woman, rather than a young man, coming of age within a Judaism so capacious, so dramatic, so intense, so interesting, so full of opportunities for love and a mystical relationship to God that it was an encompassing world of its own, in conjunction with modernity. That was what interested me: the juxtaposition of serious Jewish life with modernity.[96]

Although the novel is set in a variety of places, including Toronto, New York City and various locales in Massachusetts and Canada, there is a sense in *Preparing for Sabbath* that any story about serious Jewish life must culminate in scenes in Israel in general and in Jerusalem in particular.[97] In this sense, Rapoport conforms to Klingenstein's dictum of Israel being the locus for self-transformation. Interestingly, this also holds true for *Operation Shylock* by Philip Roth.

Operation Shylock also takes place in great part in Jerusalem; however, Roth's interests are more secular than

[95] Klingenstein 83.
[96] Lois Rubin, "Nessa Rapoport's Preparing for Sabbath: A Jewish Coming of Age," *The Resonance of Twoness: Ambivalent Faith in an Ambiguous World, Studies in American Jewish Literature* vol. 17 (1998): 25.
[97] Rubin 25.

religious.[98] The novel deals with a character named Philip Roth (who may or not be Roth), ultra-religious zealots, a Nazi war crimes trial and a theory of Jewish existence that Roth dubs "Diasporism." As in Rapoport's novel, Israel is the realm of self-transformation. However, unlike Rapoport's work where the journey is spiritual and deeply Jewish, Roth's character's transformation is comic, manic and seeks to deconstruct the contemporary incarnations and self-definitions of Jews. In both of these works, Israel is almost a fictional country — a dream world separate from reality. It is a place where the outsider, an American, comes to grapple with what it means to be a Jew.

For the most part, the young American Jewish novelists we have discussed have avoided Israel. If Israel makes an appearance in their work, it is merely as the setting for Orthodox relatives. This is true, for example, in such novels as Lowenthal's *The Same Embrace* and Pearl Abraham's *Giving Up America*.[99] Yet, given the ferment in the Middle East and the angst of American Jews regarding the tragic events there, it is surprising that few American novelists have taken Israel as a subject of exploration.

One notable recent exception is Amy Wilentz's *Martyr's Crossing*, a novel that takes place in Israel set against the intifada. Wilentz, who has written for *The Nation*, *The New Republic* and the *New York Times*, was the Jerusalem correspondent for *The New Yorker* magazine between 1995-97.[100] *Martyr's Crossing* tells the story of Israeli Lieutenant Ari Doron and the tragic events set into motion one night at an Israeli military checkpoint. In the course of the novel, Doron falls in love with the wife of a jailed Palestinian militant, who is also the daughter of a renowned Palestinian intellectual based in Boston.[101] The incidents of that night set off a wave of terrorism that pit Doron and the woman as pawns in the Middle East's ongoing tit-for-tat accounting.[102] The novel has received tremendous praise for its accurate rendering

---

[98] Klingenstein 85.
[99] Klingenstein 85.
[100] *Bookreporter.com*, "Amy Wilentz Bio," <http://www.bookreporter.com>.
[101] *Bookreporter.com*, <http://www.bookreporter.com>.
[102] *Bookreporter.com*, <http://www.bookreporter.com>.

of the details of Israel, and also for the credible Jewish and Palestinian characters. One reviewer summed up her praise as follows:

> Wilentz brings her characters to life in all their human frailty, giving us a visceral understanding of the conflict's human cost and making it abundantly clear that tragedy does not discriminate — that oppressor and oppressed, victor and vanquished, are locked together in a deadly spiral of violence and reproach that can only be broken through a mutual acknowledgment of the other's humanity. Wilentz, through the weaving of an informed, compassionate narrative, has made it just the tiniest bit harder for enemies in internecine conflict to engage in mutual dehumanization.[103]

Another novel that bears mentioning is Bukiet's most recent work, *Strange Fire*. Not only is the novel set in Israel, but also the protagonist Nathan Kazakov is a gay Russian émigré. Furthermore, Kazakov used to be a poet, but he was blinded during a torture session as a young soldier and, as he explains, "my poetic facilities atrophied."[104] Kazakov is employed, as the novel begins, as a speechwriter for a hawkish Israeli prime minister. The plot involves international intrigue that is set off when a sniper shoots off Kazakov's ear in what may or may not have been an attempt on the prime minister's life. As one reviewer notes, "One does not see Israel through Nathan's eyes but one feels, smells it and hears its cadences. And for all the suspense, the politics and the darkness lurking in the eaves, the wisdom of this novel comes from that our (lame, blind, jaded, earless) guide is endowed with such wit, intelligence and humanity."[105] Wilentz and Bukiet have found Israel to be compelling subject matter, but they remain the exceptions. As American Jews continue to focus inward, they have tended to keep their focus on America itself. When they do not, their imaginations, as we will discuss below, tend to look backward.

---

[103] *Bookreporter.com*, <http://www.bookreporter.com>.
[104] Amy Benfer, "'Strange Fire'" by Melvin Jules Bukiet," <http://www.salon.com> 17 May 2000.
[105] Benfer 17 May 2000.

Looking Backward: The Shtetl

Several writers are attracted to what Klingenstein calls "a nostalgic and sometimes fantastic re-creation of the shtetl world," not unlike the work of photographer Roman Vishniac's "The Lost World." [106] In her essay, Klingenstein discusses two works in particular as representative of this trend: Rebecca Goldstein's *Mazel* (1995) and Alan Hoffman's *Small Worlds*.[107] One might also include *Konin: A Quest* by Theo Richmond, the nonfiction work that so successfully re-created daily life in a now-disappeared shtetl that it had the power of a fictional re-imagination.[108] In this regard, we must also note Eva Hoffman's work about Bransk: *Shtetl: The Life and Death of a Small Town and the World of Polish Jews*.[109] Hoffman visited a small Polish village where 4,000 Jews once lived and interviewed the few survivors to re-create the story of Jewish life there.

By contrast, in *Mazel*, Rebecca Goldstein, a successful novelist and academic whose previous novels include *The Mind-Body Problem*, chose to create a fictional shtetl. Although Goldstein's work is often distinguished by its philosophical and scientific references, for *Mazel* she turned, as she put it, "backward in time" to Jewish Poland before the war. Goldstein herself was surprised to be writing a "Jewish" novel. She writes: "Never would I allow the accidental features of my particular situation – the fact that I happened to have been born, for instance, into an Orthodox Jewish family – influence me in the solemn business of my beliefs. And so it was that I became an analytic philosopher." However, when she became a fiction writer, it was to provide her with a world that was "against logic." To this end, although Goldstein has written several works in contemporary settings, she could not resist reinventing the past as a source of inspiration for her novel *Mazel*.

In his essay "Mourners and Machers," Bukiet also addresses

---

[106] Klingenstein 84.
[107] Klingenstein 84.
[108] Theo Richmond, *Konin: A Quest* (New York: Vintage Books, 1996).
[109] Eva Hoffman, *Shtetl: The Life and Death of a Small Town and the World of Polish Jews* (New York: Houghton Mifflin, 1997).

the shtetl novel.[110] He notes that Goldstein was castigated by David Roskies for infidelity to reality in creating a shtetl, but that is why Bukiet praises her: "The precise point of imaginative reconstruction, anachronisms be damned, is there is no longer a thing itself there to perceive."[111] For her part, Klingenstein finds that Hoffman's *Small World* alone "escapes the sterility of the genre."[112] *Small World* is set in the fictional shtetl of Krimsk in 1903 on the eve of Tisha B'av. Hoffman's novel is part of a projected five-part series that will take the Jews from Krimsk through the dispersal of the community and into the present. The second volume, *Big League Dreams* (1997), is set in St. Louis on a Sabbath in 1920, and the third volume, *Two for the Devil* (1998), takes place in Moscow on Rosh Hashanah 1936 and in 1942 in the Warsaw Ghetto.[113] By focusing on the characters and their struggles, Klingenstein feels that Hoffman conveys a truer sense of the past than an attempt to re-create a shtetl.

By contrast, Bukiet feels that one need not go to Poland to find shtetls. For example, Bukiet includes Steve Stern in the shtetl category. Stern has written a series of novels that take place in a pre-war Memphis neighborhood called the Pinch (*Lazar Malkin Enters Heaven*, *Harry Kaplan's Adventures Underground* and *A Plague of Dreamers*).[114] Bukiet describes the Pinch as a place "where a community of pixilated Jews have created what by any other name would be a shtetl."[115] Stern, like Goldstein, knows he is writing about a world that no longer exists. As such, Bukiet places both these writers in the category of mourners, for the worlds in which their stories take place "only exist on paper now."[116] For American Jews, the shtetl may well be an exercise in nostalgia, but it represents a rich component of our identity, and its exploration is as much an acknowledgment of where we are going as where we have come from.

[110] Bukiet 1-10.
[111] Bukiet 1-10.
[112] Klingenstein 84.
[113] Klingenstein 84.
[114] Bukiet 1-10.
[115] Bukiet 1-10.
[116] Bukiet 1-10.

Immigrants: New Worlds

Finally, looking to the future rather than the past, our survey notes the recent waves of new Jewish immigration as potential sources of new writing. To date, this part of the American Jewish experience has gone underreported. Perhaps we will have to wait for their children to take pen to paper – but just as we have seen the politicization of Russian Jewish Americans, we are sure one day to read their literature. Almost 100 years ago, in the first wave of Jewish immigration to the United States, the immigrant experience was a rich source of material for Yiddish-speaking authors such as Abraham Cahan and Anzia Yerzierska. These generations of Jews have also played a role in the imagination of writers such as E. L. Doctorow, whose *Ragtime*, as a novel and recently as a musical, gave flesh to dreamers who would create America's image, particularly the Jewish immigrants who would start the movie business. Ellis Island has been the subject of literary fiction by Mark Helprin and commercial fiction by Fred Mustard Stewart.

Little has been written by contemporary Jewish writers about the waves of Jewish immigration that occurred after World War II and following the collapse of the former Soviet Union. Klingenstein, who acknowledges that immigrants are "the least developed theme," mentions Johanna Kaplan's story "All-City Adolescent," in which "a Russian woman, a resident in psychiatry whose recent memory includes terror and oppression, displays a much better grasp of the mind-set of a criminal inner-city youth than her liberal, American-born supervising physician, for whom pogroms are an abstract historical fact."[117] In Bukiet's latest novel, *Strange Fire*, the protagonist, as we have mentioned above, is a Russian émigré to Israel. These few examples, though, are the work of American-born writers; we have yet to see the emergence by Jewish Russian-Americans about their own experience. We are still waiting for the Isaac Babel of Brighton Beach to emerge.

In sum, we are in the midst of a renaissance of American

---

[117] Klingenstein 84.

Jewish creativity. It is also evident that, to paraphrase Mark Twain, the reports of the death of Jewish American literature were greatly exaggerated. On the contrary, American Jews are vigorously engaged in exploring who they are, in all their complexity and variety. Currently, we are enjoying a plethora of complex and richly detailed work by and about American Jewish women, gays, children of the Holocaust and any combination of the above. We are seeing works about Judaism in all its iterations, from the Hasidic world to the Reform. There are imaginative works about shtetl life, Israel and the worlds of the new immigrants. Contemporary American Jewish writers are exploring the margins of American Jewish society, but they are doing so for the mainstream and presenting to all Americans a new image of American Jews. "American Jewish life has had its confrontation with assimilation," Anne Roiphe tells us. "The end of the melting pot dream has been reached." [118] However, American Jewish literature is not poorer for the experience. On the contrary, it is richer because of its diversity. We find this as true in literature as we do in other arenas we have explored in this volume, be it music, politics, education or philanthropy.

Finally, to return to Isaiah Berlin's contention that Jews do not contribute to culture, let us recall our biblical ancestor Joseph. Joseph in Egypt gained favor from the Pharaoh because he could interpret Pharaoh's dreams. Perhaps the role of Jews in American culture is to interpret our country's and our own dreams. If the literature we have surveyed is any indication, the success of American Jewish writers today is deeply informed by their function as interpreters of the Jewish role in contemporary society.

[118] Roiphe 51.

About the Authors

Barry Glassner is the Myron and Marian Casden Director of the Casden Institute for the Study of the Jewish Role in American Life and a Professor of Sociology at the University of Southern California. Professor Glassner was chair of the Department of Sociology for six years prior to his directorship. Before coming to USC, he served as chair of Sociology at the University of Connecticut and Syracuse University. Professor Glassner has authored four books and co-authored or edited six books; his research papers have been published in leading scholarly journals.

Hilary Taub Lachoff is the Assistant Director of the Casden Institute for the Study of the Jewish Role in American Life at the University of Southern California. She has a B.A. from the University of Judaism and an M.A. from Vanderbilt University, both in the field of psychology. Ms. Lachoff has authored, co-authored or edited several training manuals, scholarly works and research papers. Her work has been published in *Science*.

Tom Teicholz is a writer in Los Angeles, California. His work has appeared in the *New York Times Sunday Magazine*, the *Paris Review*, *Interview* and *The Forward*. He is the author of *The Trial of Ivan the Terrible: State of Israel vs. John Demjanjuk* and the co-author with Marvin Traub of *Like No Other Store: The Bloomingdale's Legend and the Revolution in American Marketing*. Mr. Teicholz is also the editor of and has written introductions for two volumes of the University Press of Mississippi's Literary Conversations Series, *Conversation with Jerzy Kosinski* and *Conversation with S.J. Perelman*.

147

Index

gubernatorial elections, 11
mayoral elections, 10
New York Association for
New Americans, Inc., 2,
18, 22, 23–24, 27
New York Times, 13, 16, 132
New York University, 21
Newsweek, 14, 15
Nicholas, Frederick, 36
Nixon, President Richard, 3
NJCRC. *See* National Jewish
Community Relations
Committee
NJPS. *See* National Jewish
Population Survey
Nuremberg, 9
NYANA. *See* New York
Association for New
Americans, Inc.

O

O'Connor, Justice Sandra
Day, 97
O'Neill, Tip, 23
Orthodox Jews
conservative political
tendencies, 2, 12
day schools, 106–107, 109
sociological dynamics, 7
Osborne, Linda Barrett, 132
Oseary, Guy, 31, 50–52, 57,
64
Ozick, Cynthia, 127

P

Palestinians, 6
Palevsky, Max, 36
Partnership for Excellence in
Jewish Education, 86
Pataki, Governor George, 11
PBS. *See* Public Broadcast-
ing Station
Peck, Gregory, 38
PEJE. *See* Partnership for
Excellence in Jewish
Education
Perelman, Ronald, 31
Perot, Ross, 3
philanthropy
challenges, 89–91
giving, tradition of, 66–68
mission of, 84–89
new players, 74–80
organizational mergers,
68–74
political contributions,
80–82
Phillips, Lisa, 31, 34
Phillips, Professor Bruce,
113–115, 118
Picon, Molly, 127
Pinsker, Sanford, 122, 123
politics
contributions, 80–82
historical support and
statistics, 2–3
at the institutional level,
19–21
Jewish women in, 19–21
liberalism, theories for,
4–7